CONTENTS

KT-371-454

	Page
Key to symbols and admission charge bands	2
General information	3
NTS head office and regional offices	4
List of properties by region	5
Alphabetical list of properties and descriptions	6
Other places of interest to visit	69
Holidays with the Trust	70
NTS Members' Centres	73
Countryside in Trust	74
Ranger/naturalist service	76
NTS Conservation Volunteers	77
Education in the Trust	78
Gardens in Trust	80
Scotland's Gardens Scheme	81
Scotland's Churches Scheme	81
Road to the Isles	84
Gift membership	86
Share your enjoyment of the past in the future	87
Conservation agreements	88
What's on in 1999	back flap
Map locating properties	inside back cover

Lady in a Fur Wrap by El Greco, from the Stirling Maxwell Collection at Pollok House (see p 50). Photo: Glasgow Museums

Acknowledgements

Editor: Hilary Horrocks

Designed by: Hazel Simm

Front cover: Pollok House (photo: David N McIntyre): see p 50. *Inset:* Glencoe (photo: Kathy Collins): see p 32.

Back cover: Glenfinnan (photo Harvey Wood): see p 33. *Inset:* Weaver's Cottage (photo: Harvey Wood): see p 59; Culloden (photo: Allan Forbes): see p 23; 'painted lady' butterfly at Arduaine (photo: George A Dey): see p 7

Origination by: Marshall Thompson, Edinburgh
Printed by: Macdonald Lindsay Pindar plc.

Designed and published by the Public Affairs Division of The National Trust for Scotland © 1999, 5 Charlotte Square, Edinburgh EH2 4DU

ISBN 0 901625 61 2

J2156/162428. MLP. 190M-2/99

KEY TO SYMBOLS

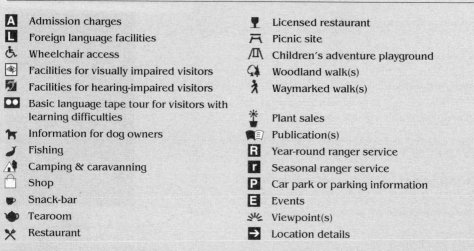

A	Admission charges	**Y**	Licensed restaurant
L	Foreign language facilities		Picnic site
	Wheelchair access		Children's adventure playground
	Facilities for visually impaired visitors		Woodland walk(s)
	Facilities for hearing-impaired visitors		Waymarked walk(s)
	Basic language tape tour for visitors with learning difficulties		Plant sales
	Information for dog owners		Publication(s)
	Fishing	**R**	Year-round ranger service
	Camping & caravanning	**r**	Seasonal ranger service
	Shop	**P**	Car park or parking information
	Snack-bar	**E**	Events
	Tearoom		Viewpoint(s)
	Restaurant	**→**	Location details

NOTES

Facilities for disabled visitors
The extent of these vary: please telephone the property before visiting to avoid disappointment. A brochure, *Information about Trust Properties for Disabled Visitors*, is available from properties or NTS headquarters and regional offices (addresses page 4).

Shops and catering facilities
Opening times as property, unless otherwise indicated. The seating capacity of tearooms and restaurants is given in brackets after the symbol. Trust shops may also be found at 146 South Street, St Andrews, Fife KY16 9EQ (open 1 Apr to 30 Jun and 1 Sep to 31 Dec, Mon-Sat 10-4; 1 Jul to 31 Aug, Mon-Sat 10-5: closed 9/10 Aug); and at BTA shop, 12 Lower Regent Street, London SW1Y 4PQ.

Ranger service
A programme of guided walks and evening talks/films is available from properties or NTS regional offices (addresses page 4).

Events
Details available from properties or NTS regional offices (addresses page 4).

ADMISSION CHARGES

Where a charge is made for admission to a property, a Band is indicated. Please refer to the key below.

PROPERTIES OWNED OR MANAGED BY THE TRUST

Band A Adult £7, child/concession £5, adult party £6, family £18

Band B Adult £6, child/concession £4, family £16 (no party rate)

Band C Adult £5, child/concession £3.40, adult party £4, child/school party £1, family £13.50

Band D Adult £4.40, child/concession £2.90, adult party £3.50, child/school party £1, family £11.70

Band E Adult £4, child/concession £2.60 (no party, no family rate)

Band F Adult £3.90, child/concession £2.60, adult party £3.20, child/school party £1, family £10.40

Band G Adult £3.50, child/concession £2.50, adult party £3, school coach £20, family £9

Band H Adult £3.20, child/concession £2.20, adult party £2.60, child/school party £1, family £8.60

Band I Adult £2.50, child/concession £1.70, adult party £2, child/school party £1, family £6.70

Band J Adult £2.10, child/concession £1.40

Band K Adult £2, child/concession £1.30, adult party £1.60, child/school party £1, family £5.30

Band L Adult £1.50, child/concession £1, family £4

Band M Adult £2, child/concession £1 (honesty box)

Band N £1 (honesty box)

Band O Adult 50p, child/concession 30p

PROPERTIES UNDER THE GUARDIANSHIP OF HISTORIC SCOTLAND

HS Band 1 Adult £2.50, reduced rate £1.90, children £1

HS Band 2 Adult £1.80, reduced rate £1.30, children 75p

Visits to properties
Parties of 20 or more, including coach parties, must always book in advance with the property, please. At some properties, arrangements can be made for visits outwith normal opening hours. Generally it will not be possible to tour most properties unless entrance is made at least half-an-hour prior to the listed closing time. Please allow time for a relaxed and enjoyable visit.
Properties may introduce the guided tour system at short notice due to the pressure of visitor numbers. An extra charge may be made for a few special events held during normal property opening times.

Public transport and cycling
In each entry for properties open to the public you will find information on public transport routes, where practicable, and on National Cycle Routes. For properties situated in major cities well served by bus and rail, we have not included public transport details. For general information on rail services throughout Scotland, tel (0345) 484950. For more information on the National Cycle Network, tel Sustrans (0117) 929 0888.
Visitors are advised that many buses stop only at the entrance gates to castles or large properties: from there, a walk through the grounds of up to a mile may be necessary to reach the property itself. Public transport information is correct at time of going to press.

Disabled and less able visitors
The Trust welcomes disabled and less able visitors. Many of our major properties make special provisions and numerous other properties are accessible. While disabled visitors are charged the usual admission price, any necessary companion is admitted free. A free brochure describing both the facilities and limitations for disabled and less able visitors is available from the Trust offices listed overleaf.

Photography and filming at Trust properties
The Trust welcomes photography for personal purposes in the grounds of all its properties, but for reasons of conservation and security and to avoid inconvenience to other visitors, we regret that we cannot allow photography or filming of any kind inside our historic buildings. Those wishing colour transparencies for lecture or other purposes, may obtain these from our Photo Librarian at Trust head office; tel (0131) 243 9315.

Sharp heels
Sharp heels damage wooden floors – please do not wear them when you visit our historic houses.

Baby carriers
All Trust properties welcome young children: we regret, however, that we cannot admit prams, push-chairs or baby back carriers to our historic houses. This is because of the risk of accidental injury to the children or to other visitors, and damage to fragile furnishings or ornaments. Children may be carried in the arms or in front slings.

Metal detectors
Metal detectors must not be used on Trust properties.

Dogs
Other than guide-dogs for the blind and deaf, dogs are not permitted inside Trust buildings, walled and enclosed gardens or in the immediate area beside buildings which are open to the public. Dogs may be exercised on leads in car parks and other designated places but must not be allowed to foul picnic areas or footpaths. At a number of properties special 'dog walks' are signposted and shaded areas are reserved for parking cars in which dogs are to be left. Please enquire at the property about the extent of facilities provided. In open areas, dogs must be kept on a lead.

Free entry to National Trusts' properties
Members of The National Trust for Scotland are entitled to free admission to properties owned and administered by the Trust and which are normally open to the public. Members are also granted free admission to properties belonging to and fully administered by the National Trust, a separate organisation covering England, Wales and Northern Ireland whose address is 36 Queen Anne's Gate, London SW1H 9AS.

The National Trust for Scotland also has reciprocal or concessionary arrangements with many overseas national trusts and grants free admission to their members to our properties. Our members are entitled to free or concessionary admission to national trust properties in Australia, Bahamas, Barbados, Bermuda, Canada, Cayman Islands, Eire, Fiji, Guernsey, India, Isle of Man, Jamaica, Jersey, Malaysia, Malta, New Zealand, Virgin Islands and Zimbabwe. For details contact Membership Services at Trust head office.

National Trust Handbook
Details of National Trust properties in England, Wales and Northern Ireland are published in the National Trust Handbook, which is available at our own shops or by post from: National Trust (Enterprises) Ltd, PO Box 101, Melksham, Wilts SN12 8EA (tel 01225 705676) at £6.45 a copy (includes post and packing).

Membership cards
National Trust for Scotland membership cards are not transferable. Members will not be admitted to a property free of charge unless they can produce their current membership card. The Trust accepts that there are many honest but forgetful members and regrets having to make this condition.

Visitor attraction quality assurance
The Scottish Tourist Board has introduced a quality assurance scheme for visitor attractions. Awards provide an assurance that the standards of facilities and services provided have been independently verified by one of the board's grading officers. The three quality grades are:

> Approved: an acceptable quality standard
> Commended: a good quality standard
> Highly commended: a very good quality standard.

The Trust has taken a leading role in this scheme and nearly 50 of our properties have been accepted. Look out for the distinctive plaques on your visits.

THE NATIONAL TRUST FOR SCOTLAND OFFICES

Head Office

5 Charlotte Square, Edinburgh EH2 4DU, Telephone: (0131) 226 5922, Fax: (0131) 243 9501
From early 2000: 26-31 Charlotte Square, Edinburgh EH2 4ET.

e-mail: conservation@nts.org.uk
funding@nts.org.uk
membership@nts.org.uk
education@nts.org.uk

information@nts.org.uk
trading@nts.org.uk
legacy@nts.org.uk
Website: www.nts.org.uk

Director: Trevor Croft

Argyll, Lochaber & the Western Isles
Lochvoil House, Dunuaran Road, Oban PA34 4NE
Telephone: Oban (01631) 570000
Fax: (01631) 570011
Regional Director: Alasdair Oatts

Central, Tayside & Fife
The Old Granary, West Mill Street, Perth PH1 5QP
Telephone: Perth (01738) 631296
Fax: (01738) 643143
Regional Director: Alex Lindsay

Grampian
The Stables, Castle Fraser, Sauchen, Inverurie AB51 7LD
Telephone: Sauchen (01330) 833225
Fax: (01330) 833666
Regional Director: David Sharland

Highland
Abertarff House, Church Street, Inverness IV1 1EU
Telephone: Inverness (01463) 232034
Fax: (01463) 713054
Regional Director: Anthony Bryant

Lothians, Borders, Dumfries & Galloway
Northgate House, 32 Northgate, Peebles EH45 8RS
Telephone: Peebles (01721) 722502
Fax: (01721) 724700
Regional Director:
Veronica Woodman

West
Greenbank House, Flenders Road, Clarkston, Glasgow G76 8RB
Telephone: (0141) 616 2266
Fax: (0141) 616 0550
Regional Director: Michael Hunter

London
12 Sherwood Street, London W1V 7RD
Telephone: (0171) 437 1012
Fax: (0171) 287 3841
London Representative:
Merida Drysdale

Properties owned or managed by the Trust and open to the public

The six areas listed below are the Trust's administrative regions and are not necessarily the same as the local authority regions. For addresses of NTS regional offices, see page 4.

HIGHLAND

Balmacara Estate
Boath Doocot
Brodie Castle
Corrieshalloch Gorge
Culloden
Fair Isle
Falls of Glomach
Hugh Miller's Cottage
Inverewe Garden
Kintail and Morvich
Shieldaig Island
Strome Castle
Torridon
Unst
West Affric

WEST

Bachelors' Club
Ben Lomond
Blackhill
Brodick Castle & Country Park
Goatfell
Bucinch and Ceardach
Cameronians' Regimental Memorial
Culzean Castle & Country Park
Geilston Garden
Greenbank Garden
The Hill House
Holmwood House
Hutchesons' Hall
Pollok House
Souter Johnnie's Cottage
The Tenement House
Weaver's Cottage

GRAMPIAN

Castle Fraser
Craigievar Castle
Crathes Castle
Drum Castle
Fyvie Castle
Haddo House
Leith Hall
Pitmedden Garden

MAR LODGE
Mar Lodge Estate

CENTRAL, TAYSIDE & FIFE

Alloa Tower
Angus Folk Museum
Balmerino Abbey
Bannockburn
Barrie's Birthplace
Barry Mill
Ben Lawers
Branklyn Garden
Craigower
Culross
Cunninghame Graham Memorial
Dollar Glen
Dunkeld
Falkland Palace and Burgh
Finavon Doocot
The Hermitage
Hill of Tarvit Mansionhouse
House of Dun -
Kellie Castle and Garden
Killiecrankie
Linn of Tummel
Menstrie Castle
Moirlanich Longhouse

LOTHIANS, BORDERS, DUMFRIES & GALLOWAY

Broughton House
Bruce's Stone
Caiy Stone
Carlyle's Birthplace
The Georgian House
Gladstone's Land
Grey Mare's Tail
Harmony Garden
House of the Binns
Inveresk Lodge Garden
Malleny Garden
Murray Isles
Preston Mill and Phantassie Doocot
Priorwood Garden
Rockcliffe
St Abb's Head
Robert Smail's Printing Works
Threave Garden and Estate
Venniehill

ARGYLL, LOCHABER & THE WESTERN ISLES

Arduaine Garden
Burg
Canna
Glencoe and Dalness
Glenfinnan Monument
Iona
Macquarie Mausoleum
St Kilda
Staffa
Tighnabruaich Viewpoint

Properties owned by the Trust and under guardianship agreements or leased to others

Antonine Wall, Central, *Tayside & Fife*
Balnain House, *Highland*
Castle Campbell, *Central, Tayside & Fife*
Castlehill, *West*
Clava Cairns, *Highland*
Crookston Castle, *West*
Dirleton Castle, *Lothians, Borders, Dumfries & Galloway*
Glenluce Abbey Glebe, *Lothians, Borders, Dumfries & Galloway*
Lamb's House, *Lothians, Borders, Dumfries & Galloway*
Parklea Farm, *West*
The Pineapple, *Central, Tayside & Fife*
Preston Tower, *Lothians, Borders Dumfries & Galloway*
Provan Hall, *West*
Provost Ross's House, *Grampian*
Scotstarvit Tower, *Central, Tayside & Fife*
Threave Castle, *Lothians, Borders, Dumfries & Galloway*

Properties owned by the Trust but not open to the public

Abertarff House, Highland
Beaton's Croft House, *Highland*
Calanais Blackhouse, *Argyll, Lochaber & the Western Isles*
Charlotte Square, *Lothians, Borders, Dumfries & Galloway*
Hamilton House, *Lothians, Borders, Dumfries & Galloway*
Kippen Smiddy, *Central, Tayside & Fife*
Linlithgow Houses, *Lothians, Borders, Dumfries & Galloway*
Newhailes House, *Lothians, Borders, Dumfries & Galloway*
Northgate House, *Lothians, Borders, Dumfries & Galloway*
The Old Granary, *Central, Tayside & Fife*
The Old Schoolhouse, Cottown, *Central, Tayside & Fife*
Plewlands House, *Lothians, Borders, Dumfries & Galloway*
Sailor's Walk, *Central, Tayside & Fife*
Stenhouse Mansion, *Lothians, Borders, Dumfries & Galloway*
Turret House, Lothians, *Borders, Dumfries & Galloway*
Wester Kittochside Farm, *West*

Properties are listed alphabetically in three groups: (a) those owned or managed by NTS, (b) those owned by NTS but managed by other bodies, and (c) those owned by NTS but not open to the public.

Further information is available from the NTS property manager; the managing body; or the appropriate NTS regional office (addresses page 4 and list of properties by region, page 5). **A key to symbols and admission charge bands appears on page 2.**

PROPERTIES OWNED OR MANAGED BY THE NATIONAL TRUST FOR SCOTLAND AND OPEN TO THE PUBLIC

Alloa Tower

ALLOA PARK, ALLOA, CLACKMANNANSHIRE, FK10 1PP. TEL ALLOA (01259) 211701.

Award-winning restoration of the ancestral home of the Erskine family, Earls of Mar and Kellie. Completed in 1497, Alloa Tower is one of the largest surviving medieval tower houses. Of special interest are the original oak roof beams, medieval groin vaulting, a pit dungeon and the original internal well. The Tower was significantly modified in the early 18th century by the 6th Earl, including the addition of a domed Italianate staircase leading to the Great Hall. The Erskines were custodians of the young Mary, Queen of Scots; the 1st Earl was Regent of Scotland; and the 6th Earl was involved in the 1715 Jacobite Uprising. The fascinating story of the family and the Tower is illustrated by a superb collection of portraits loaned by the present Earl, including paintings by David Allan, Raeburn and Kneller.

In 1988, the 13th Earl of Mar and Kellie and Clackmannan District Council formed the Alloa Tower Building Preservation Trust which, with co-finance from the European Regional Development Fund, has carried out an eight-year restoration programme. Alloa Tower is now being managed by the NTS in partnership with Clackmannanshire Council, and opened to the public in July 1996: it was officially opened by Her Majesty the Queen in July 1997 to mark its 500th anniversary. Alloa Tower is in the process of being transferred to The National Trust for Scotland by the current trustees.

Resident Property Manager: Piers de Salis.

OPEN: *Good Friday to Easter Monday and 1 May to 3 Oct, daily 1.30-5.30; wekends in Oct, 1.30-5.30 (last admission 5)*

A *Band I: see p 2 (25% discount to Clackmannanshire residents)*

&. *Toilet. Ground floor only*

📖 ⚡ **P** **E**

➡ On A907, in Alloa. Bus: stops in town centre, then short walk; tel Midland Bluebird/Mackie's Buses, (01259) 216180

Angus folk Museum

KIRKWYND, GLAMIS, FORFAR, ANGUS DD8 1RT. TEL GLAMIS (01307) 840288, FAX (01307) 840233.

Housing one of Scotland's finest folk collections, this museum presents a vivid insight into how the rural workforce used to live. Six charming 18th-century cottages contain the domestic section, and the agricultural collection is in the farm steading opposite, illustrating changes in the

OPEN: Good Friday to Easter Monday and 1 May to 3 Oct, daily 11-5; weekends in Oct, 11-5 (last admission 4.30)

A Band I: see p 2

L Explanatory text in French, German, Italian, Spanish

♿ Toilet. All main rooms

📖 **P** **E**

➡ Off A94, in Glamis, 5m SW of Forfar. Bus: limited service from Dundee, Forfar and Kirriemuir; tel Meffan Coaches, (01575) 572130 or Tayside Buses, (01382) 201121

Angus countryside over the last 200 years. One of the most dramatic artifacts is the restored 19th-century black horse-drawn 'Glenisla' hearse.

The collection was brought together by Jean, Lady Maitland, and was previously the responsibility of local trustees. The generous donation of an endowment fund by an anonymous local resident enabled the Trust to accept the Collection. The steading building was donated by the Earl of Strathmore and Kinghorne.

Property Manager: Kathleen Ager.

ARDUAINE GARDEN

ARDUAINE, OBAN, ARGYLL, PA34 4XQ. TEL/FAX KILMELFORD (01852) 200366.

OPEN: all year, daily 9.30-sunset

A Band I: see p 2

L Brief information sheet in French, German

♿ Most of garden. Wheelchair available

🍴 Meals and refreshments at Loch Melfort Hotel adjacent to Trust car park: tel Kilmelford (01852) 200233

📖 ✳ **P** **E** ❄

➡ A816, 20m S of Oban and 18m N of Lochgilphead. Bus: infrequent service passes garden entrance; tel West Coast Motors, (01586) 552319

A green oasis of tranquillity nestling on the west coast, Arduaine will surprise and delight the visitor every day of the year. This 20-acre garden on the Sound of Jura lies on the south slope of a promontory between Loch Melfort and Asknish Bay and benefits from the warming effect of the North Atlantic Drift or Gulf Stream. The spectacular rhododendrons bring enthusiasts from far and wide, and azaleas, magnolias and many other shrubs fill the garden with scent and colour. Blue Tibetan poppies, giant Himalayan lilies and Chatham Island forget-me-nots are just part of a perennial collection flowering well on into autumn. From the tall trees of the woodland garden to the water lilies in the ponds, Arduaine takes the visitor on horticultural journey across the temperate world. Reception Centre.

James Arthur Campbell began planting in 1898, influenced by Osgood MacKenzie, creator of Inverewe. Essex nurserymen Edmund and Harry Wright bought Arduaine in 1971, and after 21 years' restoration and development gave the garden to the Trust in 1992. The installation of new tourist facilities in 1997 was co-financed by the European Regional Development Fund and Argyll and the Islands Enterprise.

Resident Property Manager/Head Gardener: Maurice Wilkins.

BACHELORS' CLUB

SANDGATE STREET, TARBOLTON,
SOUTH AYRSHIRE, KA5 5RB.
TEL TARBOLTON (01292)
541940 DURING OPENING TIMES.

In this 17th-century thatched house, Robert Burns and friends formed a debating club in 1780. Burns attended dancing lessons, and was initiated into Freemasonry here, in 1781. Period furnishings.

Purchased in 1938.

Property Manager: Vacant

OPEN: Good Friday to 3 Oct, daily 1.30-5.30, weekends in Oct, 1.30-5.30 (last admission 5)

A *Band K: see p 2*

→ In Tarbolton, off A77 S of Kilmarnock and off A76 at Mauchline, 7½m NE of Ayr. Bus: ½-hourly from Ayr; tel (0141) 332 7133

BALMACARA ESTATE & LOCHALSH WOODLAND GARDEN

LOCHALSH HOUSE (NTS), BALMACARA, KYLE, ROSS-SHIRE, IV40 8DN.
TEL BALMACARA (01599) 566325, FAX (01599) 566359.

A crofting estate of 5,616 acres with outstanding views of Skye and Applecross. Traditional crofting is still carried out at Drumbuie and Duirinish, and Plockton is an Outstanding Conservation Area. Lochalsh Woodland Garden provides pleasant sheltered walks beside the shores of Loch Alsh. Mature Scots pine, oaks and beeches with developing collections of rhododendrons, bamboo, ferns, fuchsias and hydrangeas all flourish. Kiosk with informal interpretation of the garden and estate.

The Balmacara Estate was bequeathed to the Trust in 1946 by the late Lady Hamilton. Lochalsh House and policies were conveyed to the Trust by National Land Fund procedures in 1954.

Resident Administrator: Iain Turnbull.

Ranger/naturalist (based on Kintail): Willie Fraser; tel Glenshiel (01599) 511231, fax (01599) 511417.

OPEN: estate, all year; woodland garden, all year, daily 9-sunset; kiosk (unstaffed), 1 Apr to 30 Sep, daily 9-5

A *Band M: see p 2*

→ A87, 3m E of Kyle of Lochalsh. Bus: Skyeways from Inverness and Glasgow; tel (01463) 710119

Balmerino Abbey

Balmerino, Fife.

Ruins of a Cistercian monastery, founded in 1229. Visitors may not enter the buildings but can view them from the grounds, which contain an ancient Spanish Chestnut tree, one of the oldest in the country.

Given to the Trust in 1936 by the Earl of Dundee.

OPEN: *All year*

A *Band N: see p 2*

⊓

➜ **Off A914, 5m SW of Newport-on-Tay**

Bannockburn

Glasgow Road, Stirling FK7 0LJ. Tel Bannockburn (01786) 812664, fax (01786) 810892.

OPEN: *site, all year, daily. Heritage Centre, 1 to 31 Mar and 1 Nov to 23 Dec, daily 11-3; 1 Apr to 31 Oct, daily 10-5.30 (last audio-visual show, half-an-hour before closing)*

A *Band I: see p 2 (includes audio tour)*

L *Guidebook in French and German; A/V in French and German for groups*

♿ *Site, Heritage Centre and audio-visual presentation. Toilet. Wheelchair available*

Braille guidebook

Induction loop for the hard-of-hearing

Open as Heritage Centre

(60) opening this year

📖 **P**

➜ **Off M80/M9 at Junction 9, 2m S of Stirling. Bus: Midland Bluebird or Strathclyde Buses from Stirling bus station**

The Bannockburn Heritage Centre is situated at one of the most important historic sites in Scotland. On the battlefield nearby, in June 1314, King Robert the Bruce routed the forces of King Edward II to win freedom for the Scots from English domination. A few yards from the Centre is the famous Borestone site which by tradition was Bruce's command post before the battle. This site is enclosed by the Rotunda focusing on the approach route of the English army to its objective – Stirling Castle. The Rotunda was inaugurated by Her Majesty the Queen in June 1964, when she also unveiled the equestrian statue of Bruce by Pilkington Jackson which was presented to the Trust.

The Centre, run by The National Trust for Scotland, provides an exhibition – *The Kingdom of the Scots* – opened in 1987 and updated in 1996, together with an audio-visual presentation of the Battle of Bannockburn; display panels at Rotunda. Audio tour of property.

In 1930, to prevent use of the ground for building, a committee under the 10th Earl of Elgin and Kincardine, head of the Bruce family, raised funds to purchase 58 acres of the Borestone area. This was subsequently presented to the Trust which in 1960 purchased further land, facilitating access from M80 and M9 via A872.

During 1981 the Scottish Tourist Board financed a major redevelopment of the Trust's Centre, situated close to the junction of motorways and trunk roads. Enhancement of the visitor tour in 1996/7 was co-financed by the European Regional Development Fund. The provision of a tearoom in 1999 was co-financed by Forth Valley Enterprise.

Resident Property Manager: Judith Fairley.

Barrie's Birthplace & Camera Obscura

9 Brechin Road, Kirriemuir, Angus DD8 4BX. Tel Kirriemuir (01575) 572646.

In this two-storeyed house J M Barrie (1860-1937) was born. The upper floors are furnished as they may have been when Barrie lived there. The adjacent house, No 11, houses an exhibition – *The Genius of J M Barrie* – about Barrie's literary and theatrical works. The outside wash-house is said to have been his first theatre. Audio programme.

Camera Obscura, Kirrie Hill, Kirriemuir. In 1930, J M Barrie was given the freedom of Kirriemuir. He subsequently presented the town with the cricket pavilion on Kirrie Hill, and the Camera Obscura within it. The Camera Obscura is opened in co-operation with Angus Council (at times it will be unable to operate due to weather conditions). Enquiries to Barrie's Birthplace.

OPEN: Good Friday to Easter Monday and 1 May to 30 Sep, daily 1.30-4.30.

OPEN: *Good Friday to Easter Monday and 1 May to 3 Oct, Mon-Sat 11-5.30, Sun 1.30-5.30; weekends in Oct, Sat 11-5.30, Sun 1.30-5.30 (last admission 5)*

A *Band K: see p 2*

L *Explanatory text in Dutch, French, German, Italian, Japanese, Spanish, Swedish*

Stairlift. Camera Obscura unsuitable for disabled visitors

Braille guidebook

Induction loop for the hard-of-hearing

(12)

→ **A90/A926, in Kirriemuir, 6m NW of Forfar. Bus: Strathtay Scottish (No 20) from Dundee via Forfar; tel (01382) 228054**

At Barrie's death there was a proposal to remove the birthplace to the USA, but in 1937 Mr D Alves bought it and gave it to the Trust with funds for restoration.

Joint Property Managers: Karen Gilmour and Sheila Philp

Barry Mill

BARRY, CARNOUSTIE, ANGUS DD7 7RJ. TEL CARNOUSTIE (01241) 856761.

OPEN: *Good Friday to Easter Monday and 1 May to 3 Oct, daily 11-5; weekends in Oct, 11-5*

A *Band K: see p 2*

&. *Toilet. Most parts accessible*

🐕 *Dog walk*

 🧍 📖 P

➔ N of Barry village between A92 and A930, 2m W of Carnoustie. Bus: Strathtay Scottish from Dundee, Carnoustie and Arbroath, stops in Barry village (½m); tel (01382) 228054

This 19th-century meal mill works on a demonstration basis. Records show that a mill has occupied the site since at least 1539. The present building was rebuilt in 1814 following a fire. Barry Mill was the last water-powered meal mill to work in Angus, producing oatmeal until the late 1970s and animal feed until 1982. That year damage to the mill lade resulted in the cessation of commercial operations.

Now the original machinery is fully restored and turning again. Milling demonstrations normally take place on Saturday and Sunday afternoons and for pre-booked parties. The product is used for animal feed as present hygiene regulations make it difficult to produce meal for human consumption.

Displays highlight the important place the mill held in the community.

In 1988, the Trust bought the deteriorating buildings with the aid of generous bequests from Miss Isobel L Neish and Miss Isabelle Tyrie, to prevent further decay and to conserve them for the nation.

Resident Property Manager: Peter Ellis.

Ben Lawers

NTS OFFICE, LYNEDOCH, MAIN STREET, KILLIN FK21 8UW.   TEL KILLIN (01567) 820397 (VISITOR CENTRE) OR TEL/FAX KILLIN (01567) 820988 (OFFICE) (MON-FRI 9-3).

Perthshire's highest mountain (3,984ft) with views from the Atlantic to the North Sea. In the Trust's care are 8,530 acres of the southern slopes of the Lawers range and 3,230 acres of the Tarmachan range, noted for a rich variety of mountain plants. Birds include raven, ring-ouzel, red grouse, ptarmigan, dipper and curlew. Nature trail, now fenced to exclude sheep to allow the restoration of the vegetation. Regeneration of trees, shrubs and herbaceous plants is progressing. Habitat restoration work is also planned for the Tarmachan area. Audio-visual programmes with special version for children.

OPEN: Site, all year, daily.
Visitor Centre, 1 Apr (or Good
Friday if earlier) to 30 Sep, daily
10-5. (The Centre may close for
half-an-hour between 1 and 2.)

A Audio-visual programmes:
Band M: see p 2

Dogs must be kept on lead at
all times

Chairlift to first-floor auditorium

Induction loop

R **P** At Visitor Centre **E**

→ Off A827, 1½m-9½m NE of Killin,
N of Loch Tay

Bought in 1950 by the Trust's Mountainous Country Fund formed by the late Mr Percy Unna. The Tarmachan area was bought in 1996 as a result of a public appeal and grant aid support from Scottish Natural Heritage.

The building of a Visitor Centre, opened in 1972, was made possible by grants from the Countryside Commission for Scotland, the Carnegie United Kingdom Trust and Perthshire County Council. Interpretive displays were enhanced in 1997/8 as part of a general upgrading of the Centre, through co-finance from the European Regional Development Fund and Scottish Enterprise Tayside. Simultaneously repairs to footpaths were made possible with co-finance from the European Agricultural Guidance and Guarantee Fund, Scottish Natural Heritage and the Scottish Mountaineering Trust. In 1998 The Tarmachan Habitat Restoration and Improvement Project was made possible with co-finance from the European Agricultural Guidance and Guarantee Fund; National Lottery funds, distributed by the Millennium Commission, through the Millennium Forest of Scotland; Scottish Natural Heritage; and the Forestry Authority. The Nature Conservancy Council was associated with the Trust at Lawers since 1963. In 1975 the area was declared a National Nature Reserve. It is now managed with financial support from Scottish Natural Heritage.

Ranger/naturalists: David Mardon and Helen Cole.

BEN LOMOND

ARDESS LODGE, ROWARDENNAN, BY DRYMEN, G63 0AR. TEL BALMAHA (01360) 870224.

OPEN: All year

Sheep-farming area, so
keep dogs under control
at all times

R **P**

→ B837, at Rowardennan,
11 miles beyond Drymen
off A811. Bus: Glasgow-
Drymen-Balmaha then 7m
walk/cycle to Rowardennan;
tel (0141) 332 7133

Rising from the east shore of Loch Lomond to a height of 3,194ft, the Ben offers exhilarating walking and spectacular views all round. The property, comprising 5,369 acres, also includes the summits of Ptarmigan (2,398ft), Sròn Aonaich (1,893ft) and Beinn Uird (1,955ft). An extensive repair programme has brought what was a major path erosion scar under control, and walkers can help by keeping to the path surface. Reductions in sheep numbers, and fenced exclosures on the lower slopes, are allowing the regeneration of woodland and upland heath habitats. Ranger Centre. Toilets.

The property, along with adjacent Forestry Commission land, was designated the Ben Lomond National Memorial Park in December 1995, to be held in perpetuity as a tribute to those who gave their lives in the service of their country, and is to be managed primarily with conservation principles in mind. It was formally opened by the Rt Hon Donald Dewar, Secretary of State for Scotland on 11 November 1997.

The property was purchased in 1984, with a grant from the Countryside Commission for Scotland. The National Heritage Memorial Fund made a substantial contribution to the Endowment Fund. The creation of the Countryside Ranger Centre at Ardess Lodge in 1997 was co-financed by the European Agricultural Guidance and Guarantee Fund, Scottish Natural Heritage and the Stirling Members' Centre. The provision of the Memorial Statue at Rowardennan, a symbol of the link between the original 1950 Land Fund purchase, the commemoration of those who gave their lives during World War II and the permanent freedom for the nation which Ben Lomond represents, was co-financed by the Scottish Arts Council Lottery Fund. The restoration of native woodland was co-financed with National Lottery funds, distributed by the Millennium Commisssion, through the Millennium Forest of Scotland. In 1998, habitat regeneration, interpretation and the restoration and improvement of footpaths were made possible through co-finance from the European Agricultural Guidance and Guarantee Fund, Scottish Natural Heritage, Forest Enterprise and The Scottish Mountaineering Trust.

Ranger/naturalist: Alasdair Eckersall.

Black Hill

South Lanarkshire.

Site of Bronze-Age burial cairn, Iron-Age hill-fort and outlook point over the Clyde valley.

Given in 1936 by Messrs Robert Howie and Sons. 5 acres.

Open: All year

※

➡ Off B7018 between Kirkfieldbank and Lesmahagow, 3m W of Lanark

Boath Doocot

Auldearn, Nairn.

A 17th-century doocot on the site of an ancient motte. Montrose defeated the Covenanters nearby on 9 May 1645; battle-plan on display.

Presented by the late Brigadier J Muirhead of Boath, MC, in 1947.

Open: All year

Ⓐ Band M: see p 2

➡ Off A96, 2m E of Nairn, 1m from National Cycle Route 1

Branklyn Garden

116 Dundee Road, Perth PH2 7BB. Tel Perth (01738) 625535.

This attractive little garden in Perth was once described as 'the finest two acres of private garden in the country'. It contains an outstanding collection of plants, particularly rhododendrons, alpines, herbaceous and peat-garden plants, which attracts gardeners and botanists from all over the world.

It was bequeathed to the Trust in 1967 by Mr John T Renton, CBE, who, with his wife, began the garden planting in 1922 on the site of a former orchard.

Resident Property Manager/Head Gardener: Steve McNamara.

OPEN: *1 Mar to 31 Oct, daily 9.30-sunset*

A *Band I: see p 2*

♿ *Toilets*

🛒 🗨 **P**

➞ **A85, Dundee Road, Perth. Bus: Stagecoach (No 16) Perth-Dundee service, stops 200yds from garden; tel (01738) 629339. Rail: Perth station 25 mins' walk; tel (0345) 484950**

Brodick Castle, Garden & Country Park

Isle of Arran, KA27 8HY. Tel Brodick (01770) 302202, fax Brodick (01770) 302312; tel (01770) 302462 (countryside walks and events).

The site of this ancient seat of the Dukes of Hamilton was a fortress even in Viking times. The 13th-century fortified tower was developed in the 16th century and extended by Cromwell in the 17th century. The foundation stone for the main Victorian extension was laid in 1844 by Princess Marie of Baden, wife of the 11th Duke of Hamilton. Her granddaughter, Lady Mary Louise, 6th Duchess of Montrose, lived in the castle until 1957. Some furniture dates from the 17th century, with superb paintings, porcelain and silver collected by the Hamiltons and by William Beckford, whose daughter was married to the 10th Duke of Hamilton.

There is also a collection of sporting pictures and trophies. The woodland garden, begun in 1923 by the Duchess, is now home to an internationally acclaimed rhododendron collection. The walled garden dating from 1710 has been restored as a Victorian garden. The Country Park has waymarked trails, woodlands, waterfalls, gorges, wildlife ponds, a nature room and wildlife garden. Restored ice-house, display centre.

In 1958 the castle and 'associated chattels' were accepted in lieu of estate duty by the Commissioners of Inland Revenue and in turn, accepted by the Trust at the request of the Treasury.

The gardens and policies form a Country Park managed by the Trust on behalf of the Joint Committee representing North Ayrshire Council and The National Trust for Scotland, and supported by grants from Scottish Natural Heritage. The restoration of native woodland was co-financed with National Lottery funds, distributed by the Millennium Commission, through the Millennium Forest of Scotland. Shore Lodge, which replaces the former Basecamp, was funded by Argyll and Islands Enterprise (including a Highlands and Islands Enterprise 'Standards' award) and Brodick Country Park.

Resident Property Administrator: Vacant.
Ranger/naturalist: Duncan Stevenson.

OPEN: *Castle, 1 Apr (or Good Friday if earlier) to 30 Jun and 1 Sep to 31 Oct, daily 11-4.30 (last admission 4); 1 Jul to 31 Aug, daily 11-5 (last admission 4.30). Reception Centre and shop (dates as castle), 10-5; restaurant 11-5. Garden and country park, all year, daily 9.30-sunset*

A *Castle and garden, Band C; garden and country park only, Band I; see p 2*

L *Guidebook in French and German. Explanatory text in Dutch, French, German, Italian, Japanese, Norwegian, Spanish, Swedish*

Reception Centre, shop and restaurant. Toilets in castle, Visitor Centre and Countryside Centre. Parking for disabled beside castle. Wheelchair carrier to first floor and principal rooms. Electric battery car for grounds bookable at castle. Wilma's Walk nature trail is suitable for disabled. Wheelchairs available

Braille information sheets

Dog walk

➡ Ferry from Ardrossan to Brodick (55 mins) and connecting bus to castle (2m). Ferry between Claonaig (Kintyre) and Lochranza (north Arran), frequent in summer, limited in winter. Ferry details, tel Caledonian MacBrayne, (01475) 650100; bus details, tel (0141) 332 7133. All-inclusive travel and admission ticket from Strathclyde Passenger Transport rail stations; tel (0141) 332 7133

GOATFELL

ISLE OF ARRAN. TEL BRODICK (01770) 302462.

At 2,866ft, Goatfell is the highest peak on the Isle of Arran, with impressive views. Trust property (5,642 acres) includes part of Glen Rosa and Cir Mhór (2,618ft); fine rock-climbing and ridge-walking.

Goatfell and neighbouring mountainous country were gifted in 1958 by Lady Jean Fforde, daughter of Mary, Duchess of Montrose. Repair to footpaths was co-financed by the European Agricultural Guidance and Guarantee Fund through the Arran Initiative. The restoration of native woodland was co-financed with National Lottery funds, distributed by the Millennium Commission, through the Millennium Forest of Scotland.

Ranger/naturalist: Jane Barker.

OPEN: *All year*

R

➡ Access for walkers from Brodick Country Park and from Cladach on A841 Brodick-Lochranza

Brodie Castle

Brodie, Forres, Moray IV36 0TE.
Tel Brodie (01309) 641371,
fax (01309) 641600.

Set in parkland, Brodie Castle is old but the family association with the area is even older.

The Brodies were first endowed with their lands by Malcolm IV in 1160 and a Thane of Brodie is recorded in the reign of Alexander III. The castle was damaged in 1645 during the Montrose campaigns. The oldest part is 16th-century 'Z' plan, with additions made in the 17th and 19th centuries.

The house contains fine French furniture, English, Continental and Chinese porcelain, and a major collection of paintings ranging from 17th-century Dutch to 18th-century and early 19th-century English watercolours and Scottish Colourists. The house and its collections demonstrate an impressive continuity which bears witness to Brodie's long unbroken family history.

A woodland walk has been laid out in the surrounding policies by the edge of a 4-acre pond with access to wildlife observation hides. Wild shrubbery, particularly fine daffodil collection.

Brodie Castle, with its contents and 175 acres of policies, was acquired by the Secretary of State for Scotland using National Land Fund procedures, at the wish of the present Brodie of Brodie, 25th Chief of that name, and transferred into the care of the Trust in 1980. Brodie of Brodie also provided an endowment.

Resident Property Manager: Dr Stephanie Blackden.

OPEN: *Castle, 1 Apr (or Good Friday if earlier) to 3 Oct, Mon-Sat 11-5.30, Sun 1.30-5.30; weekends in Oct, Sat 11-5.30, Sun 1.30-5.30 (last admission 4.30). Other times by appointment. Grounds, all year, daily 9.30-sunset*

A *Band D; grounds only (outwith summer season's published opening times), Band M: see p 2*

L *Explanatory text in Dutch, French, German, Italian, Spanish, Swedish*

♿ *Wheelchair carrier to first floor. Toilets. Nature trail and hides. Wheelchair available*

Audio-tape tour, Braille guide

Camping ground (youth organisations only)

🛍 ☕ (32) 🌲 🏛 🍴 📖 **P** **E**

➡ **Off A96, 4½m W of Forres and 24m E of Inverness. On National Cycle Route 1. Bus: Bluebird Buses; tel (01343) 544222**

Broughton House & Garden

12 High Street, Kirkcudbright, Dumfries & Galloway DG6 4JX.
Tel/fax Kirkcudbright (01557) 330437.

18th-century town house of the Murrays of Broughton and Cally, which was bought by E A Hornel, the renowned artist and member of 'The Glasgow Boys'. Between 1901 and 1933 he added an art gallery and a studio overlooking the fascinating garden with Japanese influences, which leads down to the estuary of the Dee. The House contains many of Hornel's works, paintings by other artists, an extensive collection of Scottish books including Burns' works, and local history material.

The E A Hornel Trustees transferred ownership of the house to The National Trust for Scotland in 1997.

Property Manager: Frances Scott.

OPEN: *House and garden, 1 Apr (or Good Friday if earlier) to 31 Oct, daily 1-5.30 (last admission 4.45)*

A *Band I: see p 2*

➡ Off A711/A755. On National Cycle Route 7. Bus: McEwans (Nos 501/502/ 503) from Dumfries and Castle Douglas, stop in Kirkcudbright; tel (0345) 090510

Bruce's Stone

Dumfries & Galloway.

This granite boulder on Moss Raploch marks the spot where King Robert the Bruce defeated the English in 1307.

Given by the Earl of Mar in 1932.

OPEN: *All year*

➡ By A712, 6m W of New Galloway

Bucinch & Ceardach

Loch Lomond.

These two small, uninhabited islands, between Luss and Balmaha, were presented by Col Charles L Spencer of Warmanbie, Dumfries, in 1943.

OPEN: *All year (no designated landing place)*

BURG

ISLE OF MULL, ARGYLL & BUTE.

The exposed location of Burg, open to the full force of the Atlantic weather, together with its colloquial name 'The Wilderness', give an indication of the wild terrain of this property. Volcanic eruptions many millions of years ago formed the distinctive stepped outline of the peninsula, as the molten lava cooled to form the cliffs which can be seen today. Although the area is now almost devoid of trees, the sea cliff beyond Burg Farm retains the impression of a tree, known as MacCulloch's Fossil Tree, engulfed by the lava flow perhaps 50 million years ago.

OPEN: *All year*

🐕 *Dogs must be kept on a lead at all times and cannot negotiate the ladder*

➡️ By footpath, 7m W of Tiroran, off B8035 on N shore of Loch Scridain. Visitors' cars are not permitted beyond the car park at Tiroran; a 7-mile walk on a path which becomes very rough and precipitous culminates in a steep descent to the beach by an iron ladder. The tree is only accessible at low tide by following this path.

The 1,405 acres of this property were bequeathed to the Trust by Mr A Campbell Blair of Dolgelly in 1932.

No Resident Property Manager. Enquiries to NTS Argyll, Lochaber & the Western Isles Regional Office, tel (01631) 570000.

CAIY STANE

CAIYSTANE VIEW, EDINBURGH.

This impressive 9ft tall prehistoric cup-marked stone, also known as General Kay's Monument, or the Kel Stone, traditionally marks the site of an ancient battle, perhaps between Picts and Romans.

Given by Mrs Johnston Gee in 1936.
Enquiries to NTS Lothians, Borders, Dumfries & Galloway Regional Office; tel (01721) 722502.

OPEN: *All year*

➡️ Off B701, Oxgangs Road. 2m from National Cycle Route 75

CAMERONIANS' REGIMENTAL MEMORIAL

DOUGLAS, SOUTH LANARKSHIRE.

Statue of the Earl of Angus who was the first Colonel of the Cameronian Regiment which was raised at Douglas in 1689. The statue is situated at north edge of village.

Given to the Trust with an endowment in 1991 by the Cameronian Trust.

OPEN: *All year*

➡️ Off A70, 2m W of M74, junction 12. Bus: hourly service Lanark-Douglas; tel (0141) 332 7133

Canna

**Inner Hebrides. Tel Mallaig
(01687) 462466.**

The most westerly of the Small Isles, Canna is 5 miles long and 1¼ miles wide and is one of the most interesting islands in the Hebrides for its cultural background, archaeology and ornithology. Sustainable farming and crofting systems are carried out on the island. Pony trekking.

Canna, together with the adjacent island of Sanday, was transferred into the Trust's care in May 1981 at the wish of the owner, the late Dr John Lorne Campbell, who also included his Celtic and Scottish library. Acceptance of these gifts was made possible by generous financial assistance from the National Heritage Memorial Fund. The Trust, together with the Hebridean Trust, are renovating St Edward's Church to provide a study centre for visitors. The project is funded by the Heritage Lottery Fund, Historic Scotland and Lochaber Limited. In 1998, phase 1 of the Electricity Generation Project, providing an improved supply of power, was co-financed by the European Regional Development Fund and Lochaber Limited.

OPEN: *All year*

➡ **Ferry (no cars) from Mallaig, Highland; tel Caledonian MacBrayne, (01475) 650100. Cruises from Mallaig and Arisaig (see pages 84/85)**

Trust Representative: Winefride Mackinnon, No 4 Sanday, Isle of Canna, PH44 4RS.

Carlyle's Birthplace

**The Arched House, Ecclefechan, Lockerbie, Dumfries & Galloway, DG11 3DG.
Tel Ecclefechan (01576) 300666.**

OPEN: *Good Friday to Easter Monday, 1 May to 30 Sep, Fri, Sat, Sun, Mon 1.30-5.30 (last admission 5)*

A *Band K: see p 2*

➡ **Off M74, on A74, in Ecclefechan, 5½m SE of Lockerbie. Bus: McEwan's (No 383), from Lockerbie to Ecclefechan; tel (0345) 090510; rail: Lockerbie station, 5½m; tel (0345) 484950**

The Arched House, in which Thomas Carlyle was born on 4 December 1795, was built by his father and uncle (who were both master masons) in 1791. Carlyle was a great writer and historian and one of the most powerful influences on 19th-century British thought.
The interior of the house is furnished to reflect domestic life at Carlyle's time and also on show is a notable collection of portraits and his belongings.

Handed over in 1936 by the Trustees of Carlyle's House Memorial Fund.

Resident Property Manager: Fiona Auchterlonie.

Castle Fraser

SAUCHEN, INVERURIE, ABERDEENSHIRE
AB51 7LD.
TEL SAUCHEN (01330) 833463.

The most elaborate Z-plan castle in Scotland, and one of the grandest Castles of Mar, was begun in 1575 by the 6th laird, Michael Fraser, and incorporates an earlier building. The castle was completed in 1636 and was the masterpiece of two great families of master masons, Bell and Leiper. The armorial panel high on the north side of the castle is signed 'I Bel'. Castle Fraser belongs to the same period of native architectural achievements as two neighbouring castles, Crathes and Craigievar, both owned by the Trust. Evidence suggests that before the castle was built, the site was occupied by a plain rectangular tower house not unlike the old tower house at Drum Castle. The striking simplicity of the Great Hall and the stout walls do much to evoke the atmosphere of past centuries. The castle contains many Fraser family portraits, including one by Raeburn, and fine 18th- and 19th-century carpets, curtains and bed hangings. One of the 17th-century 'laigh biggins' now contains a new shop which stocks a range of exclusive gifts.
A formal garden has been re-created in the old walled garden.

OPEN: *Castle, Good Friday to Easter Monday, 1 May to 30 Jun and 1 Sep to 3 Oct, daily 1.30-5.30; 1 Jul to 31 Aug, daily 11-5.30; weekends in Oct, 1.30-5.30 (last admission 4.45). Garden, all year, daily 9.30-6. Grounds, all year, daily 9.30-sunset*

A *Castle, garden and grounds, Band D; garden and grounds only, Band K: see p 2*

L *Explanatory text in Dutch, French, German, Italian, Japanese, Spanish*

  Toilet

  (38) Open as castle, but open at 11, 1 May to 3 Oct

➜ Off A944, 4m N of Dunecht and 16m W of Aberdeen. Bus: from Aberdeen Bus Station; tel Bluebird Buses, (01224) 212266

The property of 26 acres was given into the care of the Trust in 1976 by the late Major and Mrs Michael Smiley, along with an endowment. In 1993 a further 320 acres of land surrounding the castle was purchased by the Trust by drawing on its 'Places in Peril' fund.
Resident Property Manager: Eric Wilkinson. Ranger/naturalist (based at Crathes): Arthur Martin; tel Crathes (01330) 844651.

Corrieshalloch Gorge

BRAEMORE, ROSS-SHIRE.

This spectacular mile-long gorge, one of the finest examples in Britain of a box canyon, is 200ft deep. The river which carved this channel through hard metamorphic rock, plunges 150ft over the Falls of Measach. The suspension bridge a little way downstream from the falls was built by John Fowler (1817-98), joint designer of the Forth Railway Bridge, who bought the estate of Braemore in 1867. Further downstream, a viewing platform provides an excellent vantage point looking up towards the falls.

Given in 1945 by the late Mr John J Calder of Ardargie (35 acres). A further 32 acres were acquired from the Forestry Commission in 1994.
Administrator: Keith Gordon, Inverewe House; tel Poolewe (01445) 781200.

OPEN: *All year*
A *Band N: see p 2*

➜ A835 at Braemore, 12m SSE of Ullapool

CRAIGIEVAR CASTLE

ALFORD, ABERDEENSHIRE, AB33 8JF. TEL LUMPHANAN (013398) 83635, FAX (013398) 83280.

This fairytale-like castle, which exemplifies some of the best Scottish Baronial architecture, seems to have grown naturally out of the beautiful rolling hillsides of Aberdeenshire. The Great Tower stands just as it was when completed by Master William Forbes – 'Danzig Willie' – in 1626. The simplicity of its lower towers contrasts perfectly with the turrets, the cupolas and corbelling which embellish the roof line. Within its walls the collection includes an excellent show of family portraits and 17th- and 18th-century furniture. This perfect Scottish castle remains as unspoiled as it was when lived in by the Forbes-Sempill family.

Craigievar Castle and some 30 acres of ground were bought from the Forbes-Sempill family by a consortium of benefactors and presented to the Trust in 1963. The property has since been extended by the purchase of an additional 60 acres of farmland providing a safeguard for its amenity.

OPEN: *Castle, 1 May to 30 Sep, daily 1.30-5.30 (last admission 4.45). Guided tours only. No coaches, no groups. Grounds, all year, daily 9.30-sunset*

A *Band B; grounds only (outwith summer season's published opening times), Band N: see p 2*

L *Explanatory text in French, German, Italian, Spanish*

🏛 🎨 📖 **r** **P**

➡ **On A980, 6m S of Alford and 26m W of Aberdeen**

Resident Property Manager: David Mackay.
Senior Ranger/naturalist (based at Crathes): Arthur Martin; tel Crathes (01330) 844651.

CRAIGOWER

NEAR PITLOCHRY, PERTH & KINROSS. TEL DUNKELD (01350) 728641 (RANGER OFFICE) OR PITLOCHRY (01796) 473233 (KILLIECRANKIE VISITOR CENTRE).

Eleven-acre beacon hill with splendid views. The path from the small car park to the summit has been extended to form the Dunmore Trail in memory of John, Earl of Dunmore (1939-1980), member of NTS Council and Executive Committee, and of his father, the Viscount Fincastle, who was killed in action in 1940.

Given in 1947 by the late Mrs M D Fergusson of Baledmund in memory of her father, Capt G A K Wisely.

Senior ranger/naturalist: Ben Notley.

OPEN: *All year*

🚶 **R** ✳

➡ **Off A924 at Moulin, 1½m N of Pitlochry. 1m from National Cycle Route 7**

Crathes Castle, Garden & Estate

BANCHORY, ABERDEENSHIRE AB31 3QJ. TEL CRATHES (01330) 844525,
FAX (01330) 844797 (CASTLE); TEL (01330) 844651 (RANGER/ NATURALIST).

OPEN: *Castle and Visitor Centre, 1 Apr (or Good Friday if earlier) to 31 Oct, daily 11-5.30 (last admission to castle 4.45). Other times by appointment only. To help you enjoy your visit and for safety reasons, admission to castle is by a timed ticket arrangement (limited number available each day: entry may be delayed). Garden and grounds, all year, daily 9-sunset. Grounds may be closed at short notice on very busy days due to the limited capacity for car parking*

A *Castle, Band J; grounds/walled garden, each Band K (no family, no party rates); grounds and walled garden, Band E; combined ticket, Band C: see p 2*

L *Explanatory text in Czech, Dutch, French, German, Hebrew, Italian, Japanese, Norwegian, Portuguese, Russian, Spanish, Swedish*

♿ *Ground floor of castle, garden and grounds, viewpoint trail, shop, exhibitions, restaurant. Toilets. Wheelchairs available*

🔊 *Audio tour of garden*

🐕 *Dog walks*

🍴 *(104)* ⛺ ♨ 🚶 ⚘ **R** **P** **E** ☀

➡ **On A93, 3m E of Banchory and 15m W of Aberdeen. Bus: from Aberdeen Bus Station; tel Bluebird Buses, (01224) 212266**

King Robert the Bruce granted the lands of Leys to the Burnett family in 1323. The ancient Horn of Leys, which can be seen today in the Great Hall, was presented by Bruce to the family as a symbol of his gift. The castle, built in the second half of the 16th century, is a superb example of a tower house of the period. Some of the rooms retain their original painted ceilings and collections of family portraits and furniture. A visit to this property is enhanced by the 3.75 acres of walled garden, which incorporates herbaceous borders and many unusual plants. The garden provides a wonderful display at all times of the year. The great yew hedges, fascinating examples of the art of topiary, date from as early as 1702. The castle grounds are perfect for nature study and there are six exciting trails for visitors to enjoy. In the Visitor Centre are two permanent exhibitions.

The property of Crathes, consisting of 531 acres of woodland, fields and gardens, has as its centre the castle, begun in the mid-16th century. It was given to the Trust in 1951 by the late Sir James Burnett of Leys, Bt, with an endowment.

Administrator: Vacant
Senior Ranger/naturalist: Arthur Martin.
Horsemill Restaurant;
tel (01330) 844634.
Trust shop; tel (01330) 844757.

Culloden

CULLODEN MOOR, INVERNESS, IV2 5EU. TEL INVERNESS (01463) 790607;
FAX (01463) 794294.

Scene of the last major battle fought on mainland Britain. The final Jacobite uprising ended here on 16 April, 1746, when the army of Prince Charles Edward Stuart was crushed by the Government forces, led by the Duke of Cumberland. Turf and stone dykes which played a crucial part in the battle have been reconstructed on their original site as part of a long-term strategy to return the battlefield to its original 1746 state. The original Old Leanach Cottage, which survived the battle being fought around it, has been restored several times and is now open to the public, with Living History presentations during summer. Also in the Trust's care are the Graves of the Clans, the Well of the Dead, the Memorial Cairn, the Cumberland Stone and the Field of the English. The Visitor Centre houses a permanent Jacobite exhibition, including an 18th-century sampler commemorating the battle, purchased with co-finance from the Heritage Lottery Fund, and a historical display.

The Graves, Memorial Cairn and King's Stables were presented by Hector Forbes of Culloden who also, for a nominal sum, sold the field in which the Cumberland Stone stands. The late Mr Alexander Munro of Leanach presented 1½ acres in 1937 and in 1959 his son Mr Ian Munro added 1 acre to this gift. In 1981 the Trust, with help from the Countryside Commission for Scotland, purchased 108 acres from the Forestry Commission. The Field of the English was purchased in 1989 with generous assistance from Ruth Berlin, the Glencoe Foundation and the Countryside Commission for Scotland. A further 16 acres of adjacent land were purchased in 1998.

**Resident Property Manager:
Ross Mackenzie.**

OPEN: Site, all year, daily. Visitor Centre, 1 Feb to 31 Mar and 1 Nov to 31 Dec (except 24-26 Dec), daily 10-4; 1 Apr to 31 Oct, daily 9-6 (last admission to exhibition area 30 mins before closing). Audio-visual show, same dates, last show 30 mins before closing

A *Band H: see p 2*

L *Guidebook in French and German. A/V programme in French, Gaelic, German, Italian and Japanese*

♿ *Visitor Centre. Wheelchairs available. Toilets*

Braille guidebook, raised maps, audio tour

Induction loop, subtitled AV programme, special AV channel

Bookshop

✗ *(80) Closes 30 mins before Visitor Centre*

P **E**

➡ **B9006, 5m E of Inverness. On National Cycle Routes 1 & 7.
Bus: Highland Omnibuses (No 12) from PO, Queensgate, Inverness; tel (01463) 710555; Guide Friday tour bus from Inverness, May to Sep; tel (01463) 224000. Rail: Inverness station 6m; tel (0345) 484950**

Culross

WEST GREEN HOUSE,
CULROSS, FIFE KY12 8JH.
TEL NEWMILLS (01383)
880359,
FAX (01383) 882675.

This small royal burgh on the north shore of the Forth provides a striking introduction to Scottish domestic life in the 16th and 17th centuries. Culross was then a thriving community, developed under the businesslike laird, Sir George Bruce, with a flourishing trade with other Forth ports and the Low Countries.

The Palace was built between 1597 and 1611 for Sir George and features decorative painted woodwork and original interiors, 17th- and 18th-century furniture and decorative items. On the ground floor of the west wing there is a collection of Staffordshire and Scottish pottery bequeathed by the late Mr William Steel.

A model 17th-century garden with raised beds, a covered walkway, flowery meads and hurdle fencing, has been built to the rear of the Palace. It contains a variety of unusual vegetables, herbs and perennials, all available in 1600.

Excavations in the Palace Courtyard have led to the restoration of a fine ornamental path and the footings of a former east range.

The Town House and The Study are both open to the public, while The Ark, Bishop Leighton's House, The Nunnery and other restored houses may be viewed from the outside, but are NOT open to the public.

NTS visitor reception and exhibition/ video on the royal burgh of Culross in Town House: shown to groups in Bessie Bar Hall. Audio tour of Palace.

OPEN: *Palace, 1 Apr (or Good Friday if earlier) to 30 Sep, daily 11-5 (last admission 4). Town House and Study, same dates, 1.30-5 and weekends in Oct, 11-5 (last admission 4.30). Groups at other times by appointment*

A *Band D: see p 2*

L *Guidebook in French and German. Video in French and German for parties. Explanatory text in Dutch, French, German, Hebrew, Italian, Japanese, Spanish*

& *Most of exhibition and ground floor of Palace. Toilet*

Braille guidebook

Induction loop in Town House and Bessie Bar Hall; subtitled video

(45) In Bessie Bar Hall: dates as Town House, 10.30-4.30

P

→ **Off A985, 12m W of Forth Road Bridge.**
Bus: Fife Scottish (No 14/14a), Dunfermline-Glasgow route; tel (01383) 621249

The burgh's present appearance is the result of continuing restoration by the Trust over some 50 years, aimed at achieving modern living standards while preserving characteristic architecture. Properties owned by the Trust include The Palace, which was bought by the Trust in 1932 and placed under the guardianship of the then Office of Works (now Historic Scotland). In 1991 the Trust assumed full management responsibility for the Palace, which was reopened to the public in 1994 following a major restoration programme co-financed by the European Regional Development Fund. The Trust also owns the Town House, presented by the royal burgh in 1975, and The Study.

Ruined St Mungo's Chapel, built in 1503 by Archbishop Blackadder on the traditional site of the Saint's birth, was presented to the Trust by the Earl of Elgin in 1947.

Resident Property Manager: Clare White.

Culzean Castle & Country Park

MAYBOLE, SOUTH AYRSHIRE, KA19 8LE. TEL KIRKOSWALD (01655) 760274; FAX (01655) 760615 (NTS MEMBERSHIP, SPECIAL EVENTS, CULZEAN CASTLE APARTMENTS, COMMERCIAL ENQUIRIES): TEL (01655) 760269 (RANGER SERVICE, PARTY/ SCHOOL RESERVATIONS, VISITOR CENTRE INFORMATION).

Culzean Castle and Country Park is the Trust's most visited property and one of the major tourist attractions in Scotland. The range of interests and activities at Culzean provides a perfect day out for the family.

Robert Adam's castle, built 1772-1790 for David, 10th Earl of Cassillis on a cliff-top site associated with the Kennedy family since the late 14th century, is notable for the Oval Staircase and Circular Saloon. The castle contains a good collection of pictures and 18th-century furniture, together with an armoury, set up in the 19th century. There is an Eisenhower Room recalling the General's links with Scotland.

Scotland's first Country Park, created in 1969 and consisting of 563 acres, contains a wealth of interest from shoreline through the Deer Park, Gas Court, Fountain Court and Swan Pond with exhibition, to mature parklands and gardens. The Ruined Arch, Viaduct, Ice House, beautiful Camellia House and unique Pagoda have all been restored. Facilities for visitors include introductory exhibition to Culzean, auditorium and information. Environmental education service and interpretive programme.

OPEN: *Castle and Visitor Centre, 1 Apr (or Good Friday if earlier) to 31 Oct, daily 10.30-5.30 (last admission 5). Other times by arrangement. Country Park, all year, daily 9.30-sunset*

A *Combined ticket (castle & country park), Band A: country park, Band G: see p 2*

L *Guidebook in French and German. Explanatory text in Dutch, French, German, Italian, Japanese, Spanish*

♿ *Castle (via lift), shops, restaurants. Toilets in Visitor Centre, Castle, Deer Park and Swan Pond Court. Wheelchairs and electric battery cars available*

Braille guidebooks. Tactile models

Induction loop

In Country Park

Details p 72

Shops at Visitor Centre and Coach-house, near castle. Open as castle

🍷 *Country Park restaurant (100) and Old Stables restaurant (36), plus snack-bars in Country Park*

⏚ R P E

➡ *12m S of Ayr, on A719, 4m W of Maybole, off A77. 4m from National Cycle Route 7. Bus: hourly service Ayr-Girvan via Maidens passes main entrance; tel (0141) 332 7133*

Culzean was given to the Trust in 1945 by the 5th Marquess of Ailsa and the Kennedy family. The Country Park is managed by the Trust on behalf of a joint committee representing South Ayrshire Council and The National Trust for Scotland and is supported by grants from Scottish Natural Heritage. The restoration of native woodland was co-financed with National Lottery funds, distributed by the Millennium Commission, through the Millennium Forest of Scotland. In 1993 co-finance was received from the European Regional Development Fund, Historic Scotland, Scottish Natural Heritage and the National Heritage Memorial Fund, towards restoration of buildings associated and contemporary with the Castle. In 1998 co-finance was received from the European Regional Development Fund; Enterprise Ayrshire; Historic Scotland; South Ayrshire Council and Scottish Natural Heritage towards the Culzean 2000 Initiative.

Administrator, Culzean Castle & Country Park: Jonathan Cardale.
Deputy Administrator and Principal, Culzean Country Park: Gordon Riddle.

Cunninghame Graham Memorial

GARTMORE, STIRLING.

Cairn to the memory of R B Cunninghame Graham of Ardoch, distinguished Scottish author; erected in 1937, one year after his death, at Castlehill, Dumbarton. Moved to Gartmore in 1981.

OPEN: *All year*

➡ Off A81, in Gartmore, 2½m SW of Aberfoyle. On National Cycle Route 7

Dollar Glen

DOLLAR, CLACKMANNANSHIRE.

This wooded glen provides a spectacular walk to Castle Campbell (see page 61). 54 acres.

During or after rain the path can be dangerous; great care is advised.

Glen and castle given by the late Mr J E Kerr, CBE, of Harviestoun in 1950.

OPEN: *All year. One dangerous section of the path has been closed. New route to be established in 1999.*

🐕 *Dogs must be kept strictly under control for safety reasons and on leads during lambing season in spring and summer*

🚶 *Guidebook on sale at Castle Campbell* 🅿

➡ Off A91, N of Dollar. Bus: regular service from Stirling; tel Midland Bluebird, (01324) 613777

Drum Castle & Garden

DRUMOAK, BY BANCHORY, ABERDEENSHIRE AB31 5EY. TEL DRUMOAK (01330) 811204; FAX (01330) 811962.

The keep is one of the three oldest tower houses surviving in Scotland. It was the work of Richard Cementarius, first Provost of Aberdeen and King's Master Mason, in the late 13th century. The original house was enlarged with the creation of a very fine Jacobean mansion house in 1619 and a later addition during the reign of Queen Victoria. William de Irwyn, faithful armour bearer, was given the charter of the Royal Forest of Drum by King Robert the Bruce in 1323. The same family remained owners of Drum for the following 653 years. Irvine memorabilia is shown in the Family Room and the house contains an excellent collection of portraits and good Georgian furniture. It is a welcoming house with the feeling of a family home, enhanced by the recent creation of the Day and Night Nurseries. The grounds contain the 100-acre Old Wood of Drum – a natural oakwood – coniferous plantations, deciduous woodland and arboretum. Within the old walled garden is the fine collection of Historic Roses.

The family presence remained unbroken until the property was bequeathed to the Trust in 1976 by the late Mr H Q Forbes Irvine of Drum along with an endowment.

Resident Property Manager: Alexander Gordon. Senior ranger/naturalist (based at Crathes): Arthur Martin; tel Crathes (01330) 844651.

OPEN: Castle, Good Friday to Easter Monday and 1 May to 3 Oct, daily 1.30-5.30; weekends in Oct, 1.30-5.30 (last admission 4.45). Garden, same dates, daily 10-6. Grounds, all year, daily 9.30-sunset

A Castle, garden and grounds, Band D; garden and grounds only, Band K: see p 2

L Explanatory text in French, German, Italian, Spanish, Swedish

♿ Wheelchair available. Tearoom, shop

🛍 🍵(18) /⏶\ ♿ 📷 **r** **P** **E**

→ Off A93, 3m W of Peterculter, 10m W of Aberdeen and 8m E of Banchory. Bus: from Aberdeen Bus Station; tel Bluebird Buses, (01224) 212266

Dunkeld

ELL SHOP, THE CROSS, DUNKELD, PERTH & KINROSS, PH8 0AN. TEL DUNKELD (01350) 727460.

The Trust owns 20 houses in Cathedral and High Streets; most date from the rebuilding of the town after the Battle of Dunkeld in 1689. Restored by the Trust, the houses provide homes of modern standards while retaining the charm of their period exteriors. Although these private homes are not open to the public, visitors are welcome at the Trust's Ell Shop, which takes its name from the ell or weaver's measure fixed to the wall outside. The Tourist Information Centre, run by Perthshire Tourist Board, has a video programme on Dunkeld. The Atholl Memorial Fountain at the centre of the Cross was restored to working order in 1993. **Stanley Hill**, a wooded background to the village, is an artificial mound in the form of a fortification, raised by the Duke of Atholl in 1730. 6 acres. Maintained by Perth and Kinross Council.

Banks of Tay and Braan. The south banks of the River Tay and the River Braan, from the Inver Road to the Inchewen Burn, form part of the Birnam Circular Walk.

The original group of houses was presented by Atholl Estates in 1954; Stanley Hill by Messrs J Jones (Larbert) Ltd in 1958. River banks presented by the Duke of Atholl in 1985. The Atholl Memorial Fountain was given to the Trust in 1989.

Resident Property Manager: Gillian Kelly.

OPEN: All year

♿ Ell Shop. Toilets

 Subtitled video

🛍 Ell Shop in restored Ell House, 1 Apr (or Good Friday if earlier) to 31 May and 1 to 30 Sep, Mon-Sat 10-5.30; 1 Jun to 31 Aug, Mon-Sat 10-5.30, Sun 1.30-5.30; 1 Oct to 23 Dec, Mon-Sat 10-4.30.

♿ **P** **E**

→ Off A9, 15m N of Perth. Bus: Stagecoach; tel (01738) 629339. Rail: Dunkeld & Birnam station 1m; tel (0345) 484950

fair Isle

SHETLAND ZE2 9JU

One of the most isolated inhabited islands in Britain. In a successful effort to stem depopulation, the Trust has encouraged and initiated various improvements, including a multi-phased renewable energy project with co-finance from the European Regional Development Fund, Shetland Islands Council and Shetland Enterprise. The intricate, colourful knitted patterns, which take their name from the island, are famous and the Fair Isle Knitting Co-operative sells island knitwear world-wide.

OPEN: Bird observatory: 1 May to 31 Oct (applications to above address).

Regular summer sailings of mail boat, *Good Shepherd IV*, from Grutness, Shetland; tel Jimmy Stout (01595) 760222: for flight details, tel Loganair (01595) 840246 (details pp 84/85)

Fair Isle has been awarded the prestigious Council of Europe Diploma. It also won 'Crofting Township of the Year, 1995' sponsored by the Scottish Crofters' Union and Scottish Natural Heritage. It is important for the study of birds, flora and fauna, for its archaeology and traditional crofting practices and for conservation of the environment. Additional crafts now include traditional wooden boat-building, spinning, weaving, dyeing, felting, locker-hooking, wood-turning and fiddle making and the manufacture of straw-backed chairs, spinning wheels and stained glass windows.

In 1948 the late Dr George Waterston, owner of the island, established the Fair Isle Bird Observatory Trust. In 1954, thanks to the support of Lord Bruntisfield, he was able to pass ownership to the Trust whose acceptance was made possible by a grant of £5,500 from the Dulverton Trust.

The present observatory and lodge, built in 1969 with assistance from NTS, provides accommodation for 34 visitors. Contact the Fair Isle Lodge & Bird Observatory, Fair Isle, Shetland ZE2 9JU; tel/fax (01595) 760258. B&B accommodation is available at Schoolton Croft House, tel (01595) 760250 and Upper Leogh (01595) 760248, and self-catering at Springfield Croft House, tel (01595) 760225.

No resident Property Manager. Enquiries to NTS Highland Office, tel (01463) 232034. Website:www.fairisle.org.fairisle/index.htm

falkland Palace, Garden & Old Burgh

FALKLAND, CUPAR, FIFE KY15 7BU. TEL FALKLAND (01337) 857397, FAX (01337) 857980.

The Royal Palace of Falkland was the country residence of the Stuart kings and queens when they hunted deer and wild boar in the Fife forest. Mary, Queen of Scots spent some of the happiest days of her tragic life 'playing the country girl in the woods and parks'. The Palace was built between 1501 and 1541 by James IV and James V, replacing earlier castle and palace buildings dating from the 12th century, traces of which can still be seen in the grounds. The roofed South Range contains the Chapel Royal, and the East Range the King's Bedchamber and

OPEN: *Palace and garden, 1 Apr (or Good Friday if earlier) to 31 Oct, Mon-Sat 11-5.30, Sun 1.30-5.30 (last admission to palace 4.30, to garden 5). Groups at other times by appointment. Town Hall, by appointment only*

A *Palace and garden, Band C; garden only, Band I: see p 2. Scots Guards and members of the Scots Guards Association (wearing the association's badge) admitted free*

L *Guidebook in French and German. Explanatory text in Dutch, French, German, Italian, Japanese, Spanish, Swedish*

♿ *Garden wheelchairs available. Ramp into garden*

Audio tour; scented garden

A912, 10m from M90/junction 8, 11m N of Kirkcaldy. On National Cycle Route 1. Bus: Fife Scottish stops in High Street (100 yds); tel (01592) 610686

the Queen's Room, both restored by the Trust. The Keeper's Apartments in the Gatehouse are also on display. The palace contains fine portraits of the Stuart monarchs and two sets of 17th-century tapestry hangings.

The garden, designed and built by Percy Cane between 1947 and 1952, contains three herbaceous borders enclosing a wide lawn with many varieties of shrubs and trees. Here also is the original Royal Tennis Court – the oldest in Britain still in use – built in 1539. There is also a small herb garden border featuring quotations from John Gerard's book *Herball* (1597). Recorded sacred music played hourly in Chapel. Exhibitions at Royal Tennis Court and at Town Hall.

In 1952, the late Major Michael Crichton Stuart, MC, MA, Hereditary Constable, Captain and Keeper of Falkland Palace, appointed the Trust as Deputy Keeper and provided an endowment fund for future upkeep. He has been succeeded by his son, Mr Ninian Crichton Stuart. The palace still belongs to Her Majesty the Queen but is maintained and managed by the Trust in its role as Deputy Keeper.

In 1970 the first Conservation Area in Scotland was established in Falkland, 11 acres embracing the Palace with its gardens and orchard, and the adjoining part of the Royal Burgh with its Town Hall, across the High Street. This, the oldest part of the little burgh, is particularly rich in 'little houses', of which some 20 owe their restoration to the late Keeper or the Trust. Falkland Town Hall was bought by the Trust in 1986.

Property Manager: Margaret Marshall.

falls of Glomach

ROSS-SHIRE.

One of the highest waterfalls in Britain, 370ft, set in a steep narrow cleft in remote country.

The best approach is from the Dorusduain car park (Forest Enterprise) 2½ miles off the north section of the loop in the old A87. Path 5 miles, allow five hours for round trip. Or, for the very fit only, leave car by the Ling bridge, N end Loch Long, for a long walk along Glen Elchaig before making a steep climb to the Falls. 7 miles. Allow eight hours.

2,200 acres given by Mrs E G M Douglas of Killilan and Capt the Hon Gerald Portman of Inverinate in 1941.

Also see Kintail.

OPEN: All year

🚶

From Morvich Information Centre, Kintail

➡ **NE of A87, 18m E of Kyle of Lochalsh**

ƒinavon Ðoocot

Angus.

Largest doocot in Scotland, with 2,400 nesting boxes. Believed to have been built by the Earl of Crawford in the 16th century.

Passed into the care of the Trust by the Angus Historic Buildings Society in 1993.

OPEN: Good Friday to 31 Oct, daily. Key available from Finavon Hotel

→ Off A90 6 miles N of Forfar

OPEN: Castle, Good Friday to Easter Monday, 1 May to 30 Jun and 1 Sep to 3 Oct, daily 1.30-5.30; 1 Jul to 31 Aug, daily 11-5.30; weekends in Oct, 1.30-5.30 (last admission 4.45). Grounds, all year, daily 9.30-sunset

A *Band D: see p 2*

L *Guidebook in French and German. Explanatory text in Dutch, French, German, Italian, Norwegian, Spanish*

♿ *Toilets. Tearoom. Wheelchair available*

Ⓑ *Braille guidebook and information sheets*

🔒 🛍 *(38) open 12.30 when castle opens 1.30*

🎡 🚶 📖 **R** **P** **E**

→ Off A947, 8m SE of Turriff and 25m NW of Aberdeen. Bus: from Aberdeen Bus Station to Fyvie village (1m); tel Bluebird Buses, (01224) 212266

ƒyvie Castle

Fyvie, Turriff, Aberdeenshire AB53 8JS. Tel Fyvie (01651) 891266, fax (01651) 891107.

Fyvie was once a royal stronghold, one of a chain of fortresses throughout medieval Scotland. From 1390, following the Battle of Otterburn, five successive families created probably the finest example of Scottish Baronial architecture. An old tradition claims that these families – Preston, Meldrum, Seton, Gordon and Leith – each built one of Fyvie's five towers.

An air of mystery is created by the ghosts and legends associated with this castle. The oldest part dates from the 13th century, and within its ancient walls is a great wheel-stair, the finest in Scotland. Contemporary panelling and plaster ceilings survive in the 17th-century Morning Room and the opulence of the Edwardian era is reflected in the interiors created by the first Lord Leith of Fyvie. A rich portrait collection includes works by Batoni, Raeburn, Romney, Gainsborough, Opie and Hoppner, and there is a fine collection of arms and armour, and 17th-century tapestries.

The grounds and loch were designed as a landscaped parkland in the early 19th century. The walled garden is being redeveloped to show traditional Scottish fruits and vegetables. Visitors can also enjoy the restored racquets court, ice house, bird hide, restored earth closet and beautiful lochside walks.

Castle standing in 118 acres, acquired by the Trust with generous financial help from the National Heritage Memorial Fund in 1984.
Resident Property Manager: Vacant.
Senior Ranger/naturalist (based at Crathes): Arthur Martin; tel Crathes (01330) 844651.

Geilston Garden

Cardross, Dumbarton, G82 5EZ. Tel (01389) 841867.

This delightful property is representative of the small country houses and estates which pattern the banks of the Clyde and were developed as a result of the fortunes made in the City of Glasgow from tobacco and industrial development.

The House (not open to the public) is thought to date from the late 17th century. The garden is charmingly simple, with many attractive features including a walled garden and wooded glen.

Bequeathed to the Trust by Miss E C Hendry in 1989.
Property Manager/Head Gardener: Donnie Calder.

OPEN: 1 Apr to 31 Oct, daily 9.30-5. House not open

A *Band N: see p 2*

➡ On A814 at west end of Cardross, 18m N of Glasgow. 3m from National Cycle Route 7. Bus: hourly service Helensburgh-Dumbarton or ½-hourly train service to Cardross station (1m); tel (0141) 332 7133

The Georgian House

OPEN: 1 Apr (or Good Friday if earlier) to 31 Oct, Mon-Sat 10-5, Sun 2-5 (last admission 4.30). Other times by appointment

A *Band D: see p 2*

L *Explanatory text in Chinese, Danish, Dutch, French, German, Greek, Hebrew, Italian, Japanese, Portuguese, Russian, Spanish, Swedish*

Braille guidebook

Induction loop, sub-titled video

Opens 11 when house opens at 10

➡ In Charlotte Square, two minutes from west end of Princes Street. On National Cycle Routes 1 and 75

7 Charlotte Square, Edinburgh EH2 4DR. Tel/Fax (0131) 226 3318.

The Georgian House is part of Robert Adam's masterpiece of urban design, Charlotte Square. It dates from 1796, when those who could afford it began to escape from the cramped, squalid conditions of Edinburgh's Old Town to settle in the fashionable New Town. The house's beautiful china, shining silver, exquisite paintings and furniture all reflect the domestic surroundings and social conditions of the times. It is worth comparing this example of 18th-century New Town architecture with Gladstone's Land, a typical 17th-century house of Edinburgh's Old Town. Video programme.

The lower floors of 7 Charlotte Square were opened in 1975. A generous grant from the Baird Trust made possible the opening of the upper floors as the official residence, until May 1999, of the Moderator of the General Assembly of the Church of Scotland.

Property Manager: Jacqueline Wyer.

GLADSTONE'S LAND

477B LAWNMARKET, EDINBURGH EH1 2NT.
TEL (0131) 226 5856, FAX (0131) 226 4851.

***OPEN:** 1 Apr (or Good Friday if earlier) to 31 Oct, Mon-Sat 10-5, Sun 2-5 (last admission 4.30)*

A *Band H: see p 2*

L *Explanatory text in Dutch, French, German, Italian, Japanese, Norwegian, Spanish*

Braille guidebook

In the Lawnmarket (part of the Royal Mile), five minutes' walk from Princes Street via the Mound. 1m from National Cycle Routes 1 & 75

Gladstone's Land is a typical example of a 17th-century tenement building of the overcrowded Old Town which grew up along the ridge between Edinburgh Castle and the Palace of Holyroodhouse – the Royal Mile. The building is the most important example of 17th-century high-tenement housing to survive in Edinburgh. Its site and the extent of its accommodation mark its prestige in terms of mercantile dignity. The cramped conditions of the Old Town determined the width of the lot on which the house was built which meant that extension was only possible in depth or upwards. Completed in 1620, the six-storey building contains remarkable painted ceilings and was originally the home of an Edinburgh burgess, Thomas Gledstanes. The reconstructed shop booth displays replicas of 17th-century goods and the first floor of the house has been refurbished as a typical Edinburgh home of the period. In contrast, the Georgian House in Charlotte Square (see separate entry) is a fine example of 18th-century New Town architecture.

Purchased in 1934 with the generous aid of a Trust Life Member.

Property Manager: Patricia Wigston.

GLENCOE & DALNESS

NTS VISITOR CENTRE, GLENCOE, BALLACHULISH, HIGHLAND, PA39 4HX. TEL BALLACHULISH (01855) 811307 (SUMMER ONLY), OR (01855) 811729, FAX (01855) 811772.

The A82 Glasgow to Fort William road runs through this dramatic and historic glen and the Visitor Centre is a perfect stopping-place for the traveller going north or south. Some of the finest climbing and walking country in the Highlands is to be found within the 14,010 acres in the Trust's care.

One of the main sites of the 1692 massacre can be visited at Inverigan, near the Trust's campsite. Signal Rock, west of the Visitor Centre, is reputed to be the place from where the signal was given to start the massacre. Ossian's Cave, associated with legends of the ancient Scottish bard, is high on the face of Aonach Dubh, the great shoulder of Bidean nam Bian. The Glencoe hills are internationally important as a geological site demonstrating the phenomenon of a volcano collapsing in on itself during a series of violent eruptions. Glen Coe is also an internationally important botanical site, particularly for its woodlands and arctic alpine flora. Display on history of mountaineering in Glen Coe, video programme on the massacre, information on walks.

OPEN: Site, all year, daily. Visitor Centre, 1 Apr (or Good Friday if earlier) to 18 May and 1 Sep to 31 Oct, daily 10-5; 19 May to 31 Aug, daily 9.30-5.30 (last admission half an hour before closing)

A Band O: see p 2

L Explanatory text in Spanish

♿ Toilets

🔊 Induction loop

♿ Details p 72 🛍 ☕ 🍴 ⛲

🎖 **R P E** 🔆

➡ A82, 17m S of Fort William. Bus: services from Edinburgh, Glasgow and Fort William pass the Visitor Centre; tel Citylink, (0990) 505050 and Skyeways, (01599) 534328

12,800 acres were purchased in 1935 and 1937 with the help of an appeal inspired by Percy Unna, president of the Scottish Mountaineering Club, and directed at members of his club, the Alpine and other climbing clubs. The added assistance of the Pilgrim Trust plus public subscriptions then combined to make the purchase possible. In 1972 the Trust, with a grant from the Countryside Commission for Scotland, purchased from the Forestry Commission the farm of Achnacon, in order further to safeguard amenity. In 1976 a Visitor Centre, built by the Countryside Commission for Scotland and run by the Trust, was opened at Clachaig. An Torr Woodland (1993) and Inverigan Campsite (1996) were purchased from Forest Enterprise with financial assistance from Scottish Natural Heritage. The restoration of native woodland was co-financed with National Lottery funds, distributed by the Millennium Commission, through the Millennium Forest of Scotland.

Property Manager/Senior Ranger/naturalist: Derrick Warner, Achnacon Steading, Glencoe, Ballachulish, Argyll PA39 4LA.

GLENFINNAN MONUMENT

NTS INFORMATION CENTRE, GLENFINNAN, HIGHLAND, PH37 4LT. TEL/FAX GLENFINNAN (01397) 722250.

Glenfinnan Monument, set amid superb Highland scenery at the head of Loch Shiel, was erected in 1815 by Alexander Macdonald of Glenaladale in tribute to the clansmen who fought and died in the cause of Prince Charles Edward Stuart.

The raising of the Prince's Standard took place at the head of the loch on 19 August, 1745, in the last attempt to reinstate the exiled Stuarts on the throne of Great Britain and Ireland. Despite its inspired beginnings and subsequent successes, the Prince's campaign came to its grim conclusion in 1746 on the battlefield at Culloden (see separate entry), also in the care of the Trust.

In the Visitor Centre, upgraded with co-finance from the European Regional Development

OPEN: Site, all year, daily. Visitor Centre, 1 Apr (or Good Friday if earlier) to 18 May and 1 Sep to 31 Oct, daily 10-5; 19 May to 31 Aug, daily 9.30-6

A Band L: see p 2

L Audio programme in French, Gaelic, German

♿ Toilet. Exhibition, snack-bar and shop accessible. Wheelchair available

🛍 ☕

🍴 🎖 **P** 🔆

➡ A830, 18½m W of Fort William. Rail: Glenfinnan station 1m; tel (0345) 484950

Fund, there are displays and an audio programme about the Prince's campaign from Glenfinnan to Derby and back to the final defeat at Culloden.

Handed over to the care of the Trust in 1938 by Sir Walter Blount, proprietor, on behalf of himself, the trustees of Glenaladale Estates and the Roman Catholic Diocese of Argyll and the Isles. A conservation agreement protecting 28 acres surrounding the monument was made by the late Mr A MacKellaig.

Resident Property Manager: Lillias Grant.
Glenfinnan Games take place on Saturday, 21 August, 1999.

GREENBANK GARDEN

FLENDERS ROAD, CLARKSTON, GLASGOW G76 8RB. TEL (0141) 639 3281.

Two-and-a-half acres of walled garden and 13 acres of policies surround the elegant Georgian house, built in 1764 for a Glasgow merchant. The principal rooms are available to hire for dinners, small conferences and other functions – telephone (0141) 616 2266.
The attractive garden indicates how wide a range of ornamental plants, annuals, perennials, shrubs and trees can be grown in the area and is especially relevant to owners of small gardens.
A 'Friends of Greenbank' group assists with the promotion of the property. Demonstrations.

The Trust was enabled to accept the gift of house and land by Mr and Mrs William Blyth in 1976 through the success of a public appeal for an endowment.

Resident Property Manager/Head Gardener: Jim May.

OPEN: *All year, daily 9.30-sunset, except 25/26 Dec and 1/2 Jan. Shop and tearoom, 1 Apr (or Good Friday if earlier) to 31 Oct, daily 11-5; 1 Nov to 31 Mar, Sat/Sun 2-4. House open 1 Apr to 31 Oct, Sundays only 2-4, and during special events (subject to functions in progress)*

A *Band H: see p 2*

♿ *Garden, shop, tearoom. Toilets. Special garden and greenhouse. Wheelchairs available*

🐕 *No dogs in garden, please*

🍔 *(40) (summer only)*

🍽 🕮 📖 **E**

→ **Flenders Road off Mearns Road, Clarkston. Off M77 and A726, follow signs for East Kilbride to Clarkston Toll. 6m S of Glasgow city centre. 4m from National Cycle Routes 7 & 75. Bus: ½-hourly service from city centre along Mearns Road; tel (0141) 332 7133**

GREY MARE'S TAIL

DUMFRIES & GALLOWAY.

OPEN: *All year*

🚶 *Note: There have been several fatal accidents at this property. It is extremely dangerous to leave the paths. Please heed warning notices.*

r **P** ☔

→ **Adjacent to A708, 10m NE of Moffat**

A spectacular 200ft waterfall in a hillside near Moffat. The area is rich in wild flowers and geological interest and there is a herd of wild goats. It has changed little since the Covenanters sought sanctuary here in the late 17th century when Charles II was attempting to impose Episcopalianism on Scotland. Sir Walter Scott and his horse were caught in fog on this land and were hard put 'to get extricated'. Programme of guided walks throughout summer. Display panel at information point.

This property of 2,151 acres, extending to Loch Skeen and White Coomb, was purchased in 1962 by the Trust's Mountainous Country Fund formed by the late Mr Percy Unna. A further 128 acres at Dob's Linn were purchased in 1972 with a grant from the Countryside Commission for Scotland. In 1998, the provision of the Peregrines in Trust CCTV facility, the restoration of footpaths and the general upgrading of interpretation and access was co-financed by the European Agricultural Guidance and Guarantee Fund and Scottish Natural Heritage.

No Resident Property Manager. Enquiries to NTS Lothians, Borders, Dumfries & Galloway Regional Office; tel Peebles (01721) 722502. Ranger/naturalist (based at Threave): Bob Elliot; tel Castle Douglas (01556) 502575.

Haddo House

ELLON, ABERDEENSHIRE,
AB41 7EQ. TEL TARVES
(01651) 851440,
FAX (01651) 851888.

Unusual for Aberdeenshire in that it is not a castle, Haddo House is proud to be the most homely of the north-east of Scotland's great houses open to the public. Designed by William Adam for the 2nd Earl of Aberdeen in 1732, but refurbished in the 1880s, the House elegantly blends crisp Georgian architecture with sumptuous late Victorian interiors by Wright and Mansfield. Noted for its fine furniture, paintings and objets d'art, Haddo also boasts a delightful terrace garden with geometric rosebeds and fountain, commemorative trees, Victorian-style herbaceous borders, and secluded glades and knolls. A magnificent avenue of lime trees leads to

OPEN: House, Good Friday to Easter Monday and 1 May to 3 Oct, daily 1.30-5.30; weekends in Oct, 1.30-5.30 (last admission 4.45). Generally guided tours, Mon-Sat. Occasionally some rooms may be closed to public view due to family occupation. Garden and Country Park, all year, daily 9.30-sunset

A *Band D: see p 2*

L *Explanatory text in French, German, Italian, Spanish*

House (lift for wheelchairs), garden and Country Park, shop, restaurant. Toilets. Wheelchairs available

Dog exercise area in Country Park

Open Good Friday to 3 Oct, daily 11-5.30; weekends in Oct, 11-5.30

(52) In historic Stable Block: open as shop

→ **Off B999, 4m N of Pitmedden, 19m N of Aberdeen and 10m NW of Ellon. 1m from National Cycle Route 1. Bus: from Aberdeen Bus Station; tel Bluebird Buses, (01224) 212266**

Haddo Country Park with its lakes, monuments, walks and wildlife. Throughout the house and grounds, personal portraits, monuments, plaques and memorabilia build up a fascinating account of the Gordon family who have lived at Haddo continuously for over 400 years. Paintings include works by Pompeo Batoni, William Mosman, Sir Thomas Lawrence and James Giles. Ecumenical chapel services most Sunday evenings.

Haddo House, with its gardens, hall and stable block along with 180 acres of the policies, was acquired by the Secretary of State for Scotland in 1978, through National Land Fund procedures, at the wish of the 4th Marquess of Aberdeen and Temair who also provided an endowment. The house and garden were opened by the Trust in July 1979. The adjacent Country Park, run by Aberdeenshire Council, was opened at the same time.

Resident Property Manager: Craig Ferguson.

Harmony Garden

St Mary's Road, Melrose, Borders TD6 9LJ.

A delightfully tranquil walled garden comprising lawns, herbaceous and mixed borders, vegetable and fruit areas, and a rich display of spring bulbs. The garden is set around an early 19th-century house (not open to the public), built by Melrose joiner James Waugh, who named it 'Harmony' after the Jamaican pimento plantation where he had made his fortune. Harmony Garden has excellent views of Melrose Abbey and the Eildon Hills and is situated near Priorwood Garden (see separate entry).

Bequeathed in 1996 by Mrs Christian Pitman, eldest child of the late Dr James Curle LLD WS of Melrose, along with an endowment fund provided in their lifetime by Mrs Pitman jointly with her husband, the late Mr Jack Pitman.

OPEN: 1 Apr (or Good Friday if earlier) to 30 Sep, Mon-Sat 10-5.30, Sun 1.30-5.30

 Band N: see p 2

➔ In Melrose, opposite the Abbey. Bus: Lowland SMT (no 62) from Edinburgh and Peebles to Melrose; tel (0131) 663 9233

Head Gardener: Norman Tait. Enquiries to NTS Lothians, Borders, Dumfries & Galloway Regional Office; tel (01721) 722502.

The Hermitage

Perth & Kinross.
Tel Dunkeld (01350) 728641
(Ranger Office) or Pitlochry
(01796) 473233 (Killiecrankie
Visitor Centre).

Interesting mixed conifer and deciduous woodlands with one of Britain's tallest Douglas fir trees. 33 acres. Above the wooded gorge of the River Braan is a picturesque folly – 'Ossian's Hall' – built in 1758 and restored in 1952, with further remedial work carried out in 1986.

By the wish of the 8th Duke of Atholl, first president of the Trust, presented by his widow, Katharine, Duchess of Atholl, in 1944.

Senior ranger/naturalist: Ben Notley.

OPEN: All year

Band N: see p 2

♿ Car park at Ossian's Hall for disabled badge holders

🚻 🚶 📖 P £1

R Details from Dunkeld shop or Killiecrankie Visitor Centre

➔ Off A9, 2m W of Dunkeld. Bus: request stop at Inver; tel Stagecoach, (01738) 629339

The Hill House

Upper Colquhoun Street, Helensburgh, G84 9AJ. Tel Helensburgh (01436) 673900, fax (01436) 674685.

The finest of Charles Rennie Mackintosh's domestic creations, The Hill House sits high above the Clyde commanding fine views over the river estuary. Walter Blackie, director of the well-known

Glasgow publishers, commissioned not only the house and garden but much of the furniture and all the interior fittings and decorative schemes. Mackintosh's wife, Margaret MacDonald, contributed fabric designs and a unique gesso overmantel. The overall effect is daring, but restrained in its elegance: the result, timeless rooms, as modern today as they must have been in 1904 when the Blackie family moved in.

An information room interprets the special relationship between architect and patron. It provides a historical context for the Glasgow Style, the background against which Mackintosh's dazzling architectural effects have most meaning. An exhibition in the upper east wing presents the work of new designers; a stereoscopic view of the main axes of the building; a demonstration of the effects of the wonderful stained glass; a selection of the original fabrics; examples of the effects of patronage; and an examination of the relationship between Mackintosh's work and a designed item which has become a 20th-century icon.

The gardens have been restored to their former glory, and reflect features common to Mackintosh's architectural designs. They also contain a kinetic sculpture given to the house by the artist George Rickey.

The Hill House came into the care of the Trust in June 1982 when it accepted the offer of the building from The Hill House Trustees with the approval of the Royal Incorporation of Architects in Scotland. The Trust's acceptance was made possible by financial assistance from the National Heritage Memorial Fund. In 1998 the upper east wing was opened to the public, co-financed by the European Regional Development Fund, Dunbartonshire Enterprise and a number of sponsors.

Resident Property Manager: Anne Ellis.

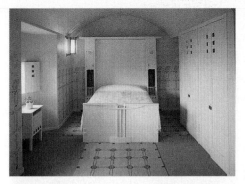

OPEN: 1 Apr (or Good Friday if earlier) to 31 Oct, daily 1.30-5.30 (last admission 5). Increasing visitor numbers are placing great strain on the structure of The Hill House, which was designed for domestic purposes. Access may be restricted at peak times and at the discretion of the Property Manager: groups MUST pre-book

A *Band B: see p 2*

L *Explanatory text in French, German, Italian, Japanese, Spanish*

Braille information sheets

In original laundry: specialises in Mackintosh-inspired goods and books of architectural and historical interest. Also Design Shop selling pieces by new designers

(32) In restored original kitchen: open 1.30-4.30

P

→ **Off B832, between A82 and A814, 23m NW of Glasgow. Rail: ½-hourly service Glasgow-Helensburgh Central Station (tel (0141) 332 7133) then 1½m walk or taxi**

ḦILL OF TARVIT ṀANSIONḦOUSE & GARDEN

CUPAR, FIFE KY15 5PB. TEL/FAX CUPAR (01334) 653127.

The present house was virtually rebuilt in 1906 by Sir Robert Lorimer for Mr F B Sharp to form a suitable setting for his notable collection which includes French, Chippendale-style and vernacular furniture, Dutch paintings and pictures by Raeburn and Ramsay, Flemish tapestries and Chinese porcelain and bronzes. The interior is very much in the Edwardian fashion. The formal gardens to the south were also designed by Lorimer to form an appropriate setting for the house. Restored Edwardian laundry. Regular exhibitions of local artists' work, path to hilltop panoramic indicator. Special events this year to commemorate 50 years of Trust ownership. See also Scotstarvit Tower (page 64).

Bequeathed in 1949 by Miss E C Sharp with 1,243 acres of gardens, forest and farmland as endowment. The present holding is 500 acres. Until 1977 the upper floor was used as a convalescent home by the Marie Curie Foundation.

Resident Property Manager: June Pratt.

OPEN: House, Good Friday to Easter Monday and 1 May to 3 Oct, daily 1.30-5.30; weekends in Oct, 1.30-5.30 (last admission 4.45). Garden and grounds, 1 Apr to 30 Sep, daily 9.30am-9pm; 1 Oct to 31 Mar, daily 9.30-4.30

A *House and garden, Band F; garden and grounds only, Band N: see p 2*

L *Explanatory text in French, German, Italian, Spanish*

♿ *Front-door ramp; toilets; wheelchair available*

Scented border with Braille captions

🐕 *Short dog walk in woodland*

🛍

🫖 *(44) Opens 12.30*

🪑 🎭 🚶 📖 **P** **E** ✺

➡️ **Off A916, near Cupar. 1m from National Cycle Route 1. Bus: Fife Scottish to village of Ceres, 1m; tel (01334) 474238**

ḫolⲙwooꝺ ḫouse

61-63 NETHERLEE ROAD, CATHCART, GLASGOW G44 3YG. TEL (0141) 637 2129, FAX (0141) 571 0184.

Holmwood has been described as the finest domestic design by Alexander 'Greek' Thomson. It was built in 1857-8 for James Couper, who with his brother Robert owned Millholm Paper Mills on the banks of the River Cart, below the house. The architectural style of the house, which was designed for a small family, is a picturesque adaptation of classical Greek. The elements of the principal elevations reflect the three reception rooms, their access and linking hallway and stair.

Central in the design is the circular lantern over the staircase. Horizontality predominates and the wall which links house and stable lodge emphasises this. Many rooms are richly ornamented in wood, plaster and marble. Thanks to investigation by Historic Scotland, Thomson's original rich decoration, based on themes from the classical world, is beginning to emerge. Much of the original stencilled decoration has been found, and visitors may follow the progress of continuing conservation work on this. Audio tour.

Acquisition of the property from the Sisters of Our Lady of the Missions in 1994 was made possible by an exceptional grant from the National Heritage Memorial Fund, which also provided an endowment fund, and support from Glasgow City Council, Strathclyde Regional Council and a number of conservation bodies.
A subsequent major restoration programme was made possible with co-finance from the European Regional Development Fund, Historic Scotland, Glasgow City Council and the Holmwood House Appeal.

Resident Property Manager: Vacant.

OPEN: 1 Apr to 31 Oct, daily 1.30-5.30. Access may be restricted at peak times and at the discretion of the Property Manager. Groups MUST pre-book

A *Band H: see p 2*

L *Audio tour in French and German*

🔊 *Induction loop*

👓 **P**

➡️ **Off Clarkston Road, B767, Cathcart. 2m from National Cycle Routes 7 & 75. Bus: frequent service from city centre; rail: frequent trains to Cathcart station (1m); tel (0141) 332 7133**

House of the Binns

Linlithgow, West Lothian, EH49 7NA. Tel Philpstoun (01506) 834255.

The House of the Binns is the historic home of the Dalyells, among them General Tam Dalyell who raised the Royal Scots Greys here in 1681. Parts of the present house date from the time of General Tam's father (1612-30). It reflects the early 17th-century transition in Scottish architecture from fortified stronghold to more spacious mansion. Important moulded plaster ceilings in four of the main rooms were added in 1630. The furniture dates mostly from the late 18th and early 19th centuries. There is also an excellent run of family portraits and an interesting collection of china. Woodland walk to panoramic viewpoint over Firth of Forth. Beautiful snowdrops and daffodils in spring.

Given by the late Eleanor Dalyell of The Binns in 1944, with pictures, plenishings and an endowment. 215 acres.

Resident Property Manager: Kathleen Dalyell.

OPEN: *House, 1 May to 30 Sep, daily except Fri, 1.30-5.30 (last admission 5). Parkland, 1 Apr to 31 Oct, daily 10-7; 1 Nov to 31 Mar, daily 10-4 (last admission 30 mins before closing time). Visits by guided tours only: groups please pre-book*

A *Band F: see p 2. Members of the Royal Scots Dragoon Guards, successors of 'The Greys', in uniform, are admitted free*

L *Explanatory text in Dutch, French, German, Italian, Polish, Russian, Spanish*

♿ *Lower floor only; photograph album showing interiors of upper floors*

⊙ *Braille information sheets*

🐕 *No dogs allowed in parkland*

🪑 ⚘ 📖 **P** **E** ❄

➡ Off A904, 15m W of Edinburgh. Bus: Midland Bluebird (No 180) from Linlithgow; tel (01324) 613777. Rail: Linlithgow Station 3m; tel (0345) 484950

House of Dun

Montrose, Angus, DD10 9LQ. Tel Bridge of Dun (01674) 810264, fax (01674) 810722.

Georgian house overlooking the Montrose Basin, designed and built by William Adam in 1730 for David Erskine, Lord Dun. Superb contemporary plasterwork by Joseph Enzer. Lady Augusta Kennedy-Erskine was the daughter of William IV and Mrs Jordan, and the house contains royal mementos of that period and many examples of Lady Augusta's woolwork and embroidery. Family collection of portraits, furniture and porcelain. Miniature theatre display and video. Courtyard buildings include handloom weaving workshop. The small walled garden to the east of the house has been largely restored to a late Victorian period and includes a range of plants typical of the 1880s.

The property was bequeathed to the Trust in 1980 by Mrs M A A Lovett. There is a tenanted farm, woodlands and cottages comprising 893 acres.

Property Manager: John Oatts.

OPEN: *Good Friday to Easter Monday and 1 May to 3 Oct, daily 1.30-5.30; weekends in Oct, 1.30-5.30 (last admission 5). Garden and grounds, all year, daily 9.30-sunset*

A *Band F; garden and grounds only, Band N: see p 2*

♿ *Toilets., stairlift, wheelchair available*

⊙ *Braille information sheets*

📺 *Subtitled video*

🐕 *Dog walk in woodland*

🐟 *Salmon fishings available on River South Esk. Season 16 Feb to 31 Oct. Full details, rod charges and booking conditions from Property Manager*

🛍

✖ *(52) Opens at 11*

⚗ ♀ 🚶 📖 **P** **E** ✾

→ **On A935, 3m W of Montrose. Bus: Strathtay Buses (No 30); tel (01674) 672855**

Hugh Miller's Cottage

CHURCH STREET, CROMARTY, ROSS-SHIRE, IV11 8XA.
TEL CROMARTY (01381) 600245.

Here on 10 October, 1802, was born Hugh Miller, who became a stonemason, eminent geologist, editor and writer. The furnished thatched cottage, built c1698 by his great-grandfather, contains an exhibition and captioned video programme on his life and work.

The cottage garden was redesigned in 1995 using a colourful range of native plants which Miller would have known from his walks around the Cromarty area.

The cottage was first opened to the public in 1890. It was handed over to the Trust by Cromarty Town Council in 1938.

Resident Property Manager: Frieda Gostwick.

OPEN: *1 May to 30 Sep, Mon-Sat 11-1 and 2-5, Sun 2-5*

A *Band K: see p 2*

L *Explanatory text in French, Gaelic, German, Italian, Spanish*

⊙ *Braille guidebook*

📖

P *Public parking at shore*

→ **Via Kessock Bridge and A832, in Cromarty, 22m NE of Inverness. Bus: Highland Omnibuses from Inverness; tel (01463) 222244**

Hutchesons' Hall

158 INGRAM STREET, GLASGOW G1 1EJ. TEL (0141) 552 8391, FAX (0141) 552 7031.

One of the most elegant buildings in Glasgow's city centre, Hutchesons' Hall was built in 1802-5 to a design by David Hamilton. It incorporates on its frontage the statues, from an earlier building of 1641, of the founders of Hutchesons' Hospital, George and Thomas Hutcheson.

A major reconstruction in 1876 by John Baird heightened the Hall and provided an impressive staircase. The interior is hung with portraits of Glasgow worthies. Visitor Centre and information room with a 10-minute audio-visual presentation, *Glasgow's Merchant City*. Exhibitions: *On the Tiles*, about decorative art of the tenement, 24 April-23 May. *Soft City*, new textile art inspired by Glasgow's built environment, 23 Aug-24 Sep. The Hall is available for hire for concerts, exhibitions, dinners, small conferences and other functions.

The acquisition of the building in 1982 was made possible by use of the Trust's Golden Jubilee Appeal Fund. A public appeal was also launched to enable the interior to be restored, and donations towards this appeal can be sent to the Trust. The refurbishment of the building was completed in 1987.

Property Manager: Carla Sparrow.

OPEN: *Information Centre and function hall, all year (except public holidays and 24 Dec to 6 Jan), Mon-Sat 10-5 (hall on view subject to functions in progress).*

A *Free*

♿ *Wheelchair lift to first floor. Toilet*

🛍

➡ **Ingram Street, near SE corner of George Square. 1m from National Cycle Routes 7 & 75**

Inveresk Lodge Garden

24 Inveresk Village, Musselburgh, East Lothian, EH21 7TE.

This attractive terraced garden is located in the historic village of Inveresk. It is dominated by a fine Edwardian conservatory with interpretation, and the informal garden includes many plants with the Royal Horticultural Society's Award of Garden Merit. There are distant views of the Pentland Hills and the garden provides the setting for the 17th-century Inveresk Lodge (not open to the public), the oldest house in the village.

Presented to the Trust in 1959 by Mrs Helen E Brunton.

Property Manager: Clare Reaney. Enquiries to NTS Lothians, Borders, Dumfries & Galloway Regional Office; tel Peebles (01721) 722502.

OPEN: *1 Apr to 31 Oct, Mon-Fri 10-4.30, Sat/Sun 2-5; 1 Nov to 31 Mar, Mon-Fri 10-4.30, Sun 2-5*

A *Band N: see p 2*

♿ *Path to and inside conservatory*

P *Cars may only be parked by garden wall*

E

➡ **A6124, S of Musselburgh, 6m E of Edinburgh. Bus: Lothian Region Transport (Nos 15/44) from Edinburgh city centre, tel (0131) 555 6363**

Inverewe Garden

Poolewe, Ross-shire, IV22 2LQ.
Tel Poolewe (01445) 781200,
fax (01445) 781497.

This outstanding climatically-favoured garden is impressively set on a peninsula on the shores of Loch Ewe. It is an oasis of colour and fertility where exotic plants from many countries flourish on a latitude more northerly than Moscow and give an almost continual display of colour throughout the year. Himalayan rhododendrons, Tasmanian eucalypts and many Chilean and South African plants are featured, together with a large collection of New Zealand plants including the National Collection of the genus *Olearia*. The explanation of this profusion is the effect of the North Atlantic Drift or Gulf Stream which brings warm currents to the shores of the sea-loch. Visitor Centre.

The garden was begun by Osgood Hanbury Mackenzie in 1862 and his work was carried on by his daughter Mrs Mairi T Sawyer who gave the garden to the Trust in 1952 with an endowment for its upkeep.

Resident Administrator at Inverewe and for Corrieshalloch: Keith Gordon, Inverewe House. Ranger/naturalist: May-August only.

OPEN: *Garden, 15 Mar to 31 Oct, daily 9.30am-9pm; 1 Nov to 14 Mar, daily 9.30-5. Visitor Centre, 15 Mar to 31 Oct, daily 9.30-5.30. Guided garden walks 15 Apr to 15 Sep, Mon-Fri at 1.30*

A *Band C: see p 2*

L *Guidebook in French and German; exhibition text in French, Gaelic, German, Italian*

♿ *Garden, greenhouse, restaurant. Toilets. Wheelchairs available*

🐕 *No dogs in garden. No shaded car parking*

🎣 *Available on one hill loch; brown trout. Members £5.00 per rod per day, plus £4.00 per boat if used. Non-Members £6.00 per rod per day, plus £4.50 per boat, if used*

🛍 *(180) Built with co-finance from the European Regional Development Fund; open dates as Visitor Centre, 10-5*

🌱 📖 **r** **P**

➡ **On A832, by Poolewe, 6m NE of Gairloch**

Iona

SW of Mull, Argyll and Bute.

OPEN: *All year*

A *Payable at Abbey (not NTS), including to Trust members*

🚫

🛍 *(Not NTS)*

✖ *(Not NTS)*

📖

➡ **Ferry (no cars) from Fionnphort, Isle of Mull (A849). Ferry to Mull (Craignure) from Oban;** *tel Caledonian Macbrayne, (01475) 650100. Day excursions in summer, see pages 84/85*

Iona is a small, fertile crofting island, currently inhabited by around 130 people. The Trust works in partnership with the local community and other organisations to carry out a range of conservation projects on the island. For many centuries it has been an island of special significance for all Christians. In AD 563 Columba and his followers arrived here from Ireland to extend in Scotland and the north of England the gospel which had first been introduced by St Ninian at Whithorn in AD 397.

In the Trust's care, since December 1979, are 2,250 acres of the island. The Abbey, other sacred buildings and historic sites were conveyed by the 8th Duke of Argyll in 1899 to the Iona Cathedral Trustees and are not owned by the Trust. Acceptance, at the request of the Secretary of State for Scotland, was made possible by the generosity of the Hugh Fraser Foundation. The Foundation made available funds to buy the island from the Trustees of the 10th Duke of Argyll as a gift to the nation in memory of the late Lord Fraser of Allander and provided the Trust with an endowment.

No resident Property Manager. Enquiries to NTS Argyll, Lochaber & the Western Isles Regional Office; tel Oban (01631) 570000.

Kellie Castle & Garden

PITTENWEEM, FIFE KY10 2RF. TEL ARNCROACH (01333) 720271, FAX (01333) 720326.

OPEN: *Castle, Good Friday to Easter Monday and 1 May to 3 Oct, daily 1.30-5.30; weekends in Oct, 1.30-5.30 (last admission 4.45). Garden and grounds, all year, daily 9.30-sunset*

A *Castle and garden, Band F; garden and grounds only, Band N: see p 2*

L *Explanatory text in French, German, Italian, Japanese, Spanish, Swedish*

♿ *Garden and ground floor of castle. Wheelchair available*

Video induction loop

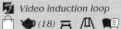

P **E**

→ *On B9171, 3m NNW of Pittenweem. Bus: limited service passes close to castle drive; tel Fife Scottish (01333) 426038*

Kellie Castle is a very fine example of the domestic architecture of Lowland Scotland. The oldest part is believed to date from 1360, but the building in its present form is mainly 16th- and early 17th-century and was completed about 1606. Sympathetically restored by the Lorimer family around 1878, it contains magnificent plaster ceilings, painted panelling and furniture designed by Sir Robert Lorimer.
The layout of the organic walled garden is late Victorian and contains a fine collection of old-fashioned roses, fruit trees and herbaceous plants. Lorimer exhibition in summerhouse, video.

The castle, garden (restored by Mr and Mrs Hew Lorimer and the Trust) and 16 acres were purchased in 1970 by a grant from the Secretary of State for Scotland, with assistance from the Pilgrim Trust and from an anonymous life member of The National Trust for Scotland. The main contents were also acquired for the nation by the Secretary of State for Scotland and given into the care of the Trust. In 1998 the purchase of Lorimer family artifacts was made possible by co-finance from the Heritage Lottery Fund and the National Museums of Scotland National Fund for Aquisitions.
Resident Property Manager: Michael Ford.

Killiecrankie

Pitlochry, Perth & Kinross, PH16 5LG. Tel Pitlochry (01796) 473233 (Visitor Centre).

OPEN: *Site, all year, daily. Visitor Centre, 1 Apr (or Good Friday if earlier) to 31 Oct, daily 10-5.30*

A Band N: see p 2

L Guidebook in French and German. Explanatory text in Danish, French, Gaelic, German, Italian, Japanese, Swedish

Braille guidebook

Toilet

R P E

→ B8079, 3m N of Pitlochry. On National Cycle Route 7. Bus: Elizabeth Yule local service from Pitlochry; tel (01796) 472290

On 27 July 1689, the Pass of Killiecrankie echoed with the sound of battle cries and gunfire when, nearby, a Jacobite army led by 'Bonnie Dundee' defeated the government forces under General Hugh Mackay. One soldier evaded capture by making a spectacular jump across the River Garry at Soldier's Leap.

The spectacular wooded gorge, much admired by Queen Victoria in 1844, is tranquil now, and is designated a Site of Special Scientific Interest because it is a fine example of an oak and mixed deciduous woodland.

The Visitor Centre exhibition features the battle, natural history and ranger services. In the Centre, visitors can now watch birds nesting, via a remote camera in the woodlands.

The 40 acres of the Pass of Killiecrankie, formerly part of the estate of Faskally, came to the Trust in 1947 by a gift from Mrs Edith Foster.

Property Manager and senior ranger/naturalist: Ben Notley; tel/fax Pitlochry (01796) 473233 (Killiecrankie Visitor Centre) or Dunkeld (01350) 728641 (Ranger Office).

Kintail & Morvich

Morvich Farm, Inverinate, Kyle, Ross-shire IV40 8HQ.
Tel Glenshiel (01599) 511231, fax (01599) 511417.

A magnificent stretch of West Highland scenery, the 17,422-acre estate includes the Falls of Glomach and the Five Sisters of Kintail (four of them over 3,000ft). There is a Countryside Centre at Morvich Farm, off A87, which is also the best access point to the mountains. Site of Battle of Glen Shiel (1719), approx 5m E of village beside main road. Morvich outdoor centre: hostel accommodation.

Purchased by the Trust in 1944 with funds provided by the late Mr Percy Unna. Restoration of the native woodland was co-financed with National Lottery funds, distributed by the Millennium Commission through the Millennium Forest of Scotland.

Resident Property Manager and ranger/naturalist: Willie Fraser.

OPEN: *Estate, all year, daily. Countryside Centre at Morvich (unstaffed): 1 May to 30 Sep, daily 9am to 10pm*

A *Band N: see p 2*

Morvich Caravan Site: details p 72

R

➔ N of A87, 16m E of Kyle of Lochalsh. Bus: Skyeways from Inverness and Glasgow; tel (01463) 710119

Leith Hall & Garden

HUNTLY, ABERDEENSHIRE, AB54 4NQ. TEL KENNETHMONT (01464) 831216, FAX (01464) 831594.

Leith Hall is at the centre of a 286-acre estate which was the home of the head of the Leith family from 1650. The house contains personal possessions of successive lairds, most of whom followed a tradition of military service. Exhibition – *For Crown and Country: the Military Lairds of Leith Hall.*

The six-acre garden features extensive herbaceous borders and a fine collection of alpines and primulas in the rock garden. There are two ponds and a bird observation hide. Unique 18th-century stables, ice house.

Given by the late The Hon Mrs Leith-Hay in 1945. In 1984, for the first time, all four wings of the house at first-floor level around the central courtyard were opened up to the public. This redevelopment was made possible by financial assistance from sources including the Scottish Tourist Board, and the Trust's Banff and Moray Members' Centre.

Resident Property Manager: Vacant.
Ranger/naturalist (based at Crathes): Arthur Martin; tel Crathes (01330) 844651.

OPEN: *Good Friday to Easter Monday and 1 May to 3 Oct, daily 1.30-5.30; weekends in Oct, 1.30-5.30 (last admission 4.45). Garden and grounds, all year, daily 9.30-sunset*

A *Band D; garden and grounds only, Band K: see p 2*

L *Explanatory text in Dutch, French, German, Italian, Spanish*

♿ *Toilet. Ground floor of house, tearoom, trail beside pond. Wheelchair available*

🐶 (28) ⋔ 🧍 📖 **Γ P E**

➔ On B9002, 1m W of Kennethmont and 34m NW of Aberdeen. Bus: infrequent service; tel Bluebird Buses (01224) 212266

Linn of Tummel

OPEN: All year

P At Garry Bridge

➔ B8019, 2½m NW of Pitlochry. On National Cycle Route 7. Bus: Elizabeth Yule local service from Pitlochry; tel (01796) 472215

PERTH & KINROSS. TEL PITLOCHRY (01796) 473233 (KILLIECRANKIE VISITOR CENTRE) OR DUNKELD (01350) 728641 (RANGER OFFICE).

Characteristic of the beauty of the Perthshire Highlands, the Linn of Tummel comprises 56 acres by the banks of the Rivers Tummel and Garry and is adjacent to the Trust's Killiecrankie property. A path through mixed woodland leads to the Linn of Tummel. An obelisk commemorates a visit by Queen Victoria in 1844.

At that time the Tummel made a plunging fall to join the Garry. The fall became the Linn (Gaelic – *Linne*, a pool) when the level of both rivers was raised in 1950 by the creation of Loch Faskally in a hydro-electric scheme. Beside the Linn is a very early example of a fish-pass which previously had enabled salmon to bypass the falls.

Given by the late Dr G F Barbour of Bonskeid in 1944.

Senior ranger/naturalist: Ben Notley.

Macquarie Mausoleum

GRULINE, ISLE OF MULL, ARGYLL & BUTE.

The Mausoleum is not Trust property but the Trust has, since 1963, managed it on behalf of the National Trust of Australia (New South Wales). Lachlan Macquarie, who was born nearby at Ulva Ferry in 1761, died in 1824 after distinguished service as Governor of New South Wales and was known as 'the father of Australia'. The Mausoleum is on the Gruline estate, which he owned.

OPEN: All year: for information contact NTS Argyll, Lochaber & the Western Isles Regional Office, tel Oban (01631) 570000

➔ Off B8035

Malleny Garden

BALERNO, EDINBURGH, EH14 7AF. TEL (0131) 449 2283 (OFFICE HOURS ONLY).

This three-acre walled garden has a delightful collection of old-fashioned roses and fine herbaceous borders, and also houses the National Bonsai Collection for Scotland. A particular feature of the garden is the four 400-year-old clipped yew trees, but there is also extensive

OPEN: Garden, 1 Apr to 31 Oct, daily 9.30-7; 1 Nov to 31 Mar, daily 9.30-4. Georgian Rooms open Suns 9 May, 13 Jun, 11 Jul, 1 Aug, 12 Sep

A *Band N: see p 2*

  Garden

→ Off Lanark Road (A70). 1m from National Cycle Route 75. Bus: Lothian Region Transport (No 44) from Edinburgh city centre; tel (0131) 555 6363

woodland for a peaceful stroll. The 17th-century house situated in the garden was built for Sir James Murray of Kilbaberton around 1635. its two Georgian reception rooms added in 1823 are opened by the Friends of Malleny on occasion during the summer.

Presented to the Trust with an endowment by the late Mrs Gore-Browne Henderson in 1968.

Head Gardener: Philip Deacon.

MAR LODGE ESTATE

ESTATE OFFICE, MAR LODGE, BRAEMAR, ABERDEENSHIRE AB35 5YJ.
TEL BRAEMAR (013397) 41433, FAX (013397) 41432

OPEN: Estate, all year, daily. Special 'open days' for Lodge and Ballroom: further information from property

R

→ 5m W of Braemar. Access from A93 via an unclassified road. Bus: Aberdeen-Braemar and infrequent seasonal service Pitlochry-Braemar; tel Bluebird Buses, (01224) 212266

The 77,500-acre estate is part of the core area of the Cairngorms, internationally recognised as the most important nature conservation landscape in the British Isles. The estate contains four of the five highest mountains in the UK. It includes the upper watershed of the River Dee and remnant Caledonian pine forest of national importance. Some 17,500 acres lie within the Cairngorms National Nature Reserve. Large parts of the estate are designated as Sites of Special

Scientific Interest and the majority of it is within National Scenic Areas. The outstanding wildlife and birdlife on this prime example of a Highland estate are characteristic of the northern mountainous areas of Britain. Conservation work here includes reducing the red deer population to allow regeneration of the native Caledonian pine forest. There is pedestrian access to all the estate, including short- and long-distance walks, but no special facilities.

Acquisition in June 1995 was made possible by the generosity of the National Heritage Memorial Fund through the Heritage Lottery Fund and continuing support from Scottish Natural Heritage. Phase 1 of a development programme was co-financed by the European Agricultural Guidance and Guarantee Fund. In 1998 co-finance from the same source and Scottish Natural Heritage enabled Phase 2 to progress.

Property Manager: Alister Clunas.
Ranger Service: Peter Holden and Phil Glennie; tel Braemar (013397) 41669.
Lodge caretaker: Sandra Dempster; tel Braemar (013397) 41427, fax (013397) 41922.

OPEN: *Easter weekend and 1 May to 30 Sep, Wed and Sun 2-4.*

A *Admission free*

➔ **A91, in Menstrie, 5m NE of Stirling**

ꟿenstrie Castle

MENSTRIE, CLACKMANNANSHIRE.

The castle is not Trust property but the Trust, in co-operation with the then Clackmannanshire County Council, played a large part in saving it from demolition. It was the birthplace of Sir William Alexander, James VI's Lieutenant for the Plantation of Nova Scotia, and an exhibition in the Nova Scotia Commemoration Room tells the story of this ill-fated scheme.

Staffed by Clackmannanshire Council: tel (01259) 213131.

ꟿoirlanich Longhouse

NEAR KILLIN, STIRLING.

OPEN: *Easter Sunday and 1 May to 30 Sep, Wed and Sun 2-5*

A *Band L: see p 2*

P *Limited car parking; access unsuitable for coaches*

➔ **On Glen Lochay Road, off A827, 1m NW of Killin.**
1m from National Cycle Route 7

An outstanding example of traditional cruck frame cottage and byre, dating from the mid-19th century. The building has been little altered and retains many of its original features, such as the 'hingin' lum' and box beds. Moirlanich was home to at least three generations of the Robertson family; the last member left in 1968.

The cottage is furnished according to archaeological evidence. A small adjacent shed displays a rare collection of working and 'Sunday best' clothes found in the Longhouse, and an exhibition interprets the history and restoration of the building.

Purchased in 1992 following a generous donation in memory of the late Sheriff Prain, from his family.

No Resident Property Manager: staffed by volunteers from Killin Heritage Society. Enquiries to Yvonne MacPherson, Property Supervisor, NTS Office, Lynedoch, Main Street, Killin, FK21 8UW; tel/fax (01567) 820988 (Mon-Fri 9-3).

Murray Isles

Dumfries & Galloway.

Two small uninhabited islands in the Islands of Fleet, Wigtown Bay, off Carrick Point.

Gifted to the Trust in 1991 by the late Mrs Murray Usher of Cally OBE, who wished to protect the lands of the former Cally Estate within the Fleet Valley National Scenic Area and who, from 1943, entered into a series of Conservation Agreements with the Trust to cover 12,750 acres of coastline and countryside.

OPEN: All year

➡ Off Gatehouse of Fleet, off A75

Pitmedden Garden

Ellon, Aberdeenshire, AB41 7PD. Tel Udny (01651) 842352, fax (01651) 843188.

The centrepiece of this property is the Great Garden, originally laid out in 1675 by Sir Alexander Seton, 1st Baronet of Pitmedden. In the 1950s re-creation of the elaborate floral designs under the guidance of the late Dr James Richardson, three of the formal parterres were taken from designs possibly used in the gardens at the Palace of Holyroodhouse, Edinburgh in 1647. The fourth parterre is a heraldic design based on Sir Alexander's coat-of-arms.
On the 100-acre estate is the **Museum of Farming Life**, Visitor Centre, herb and wildlife gardens.

The property was given to the Trust in 1952 with an endowment by the late Major James Keith.
In 1978 the trustees of the late Mr William Cook of Little Meldrum, Tarves, gave to the Trust a collection of agricultural and domestic artifacts, now part of the Museum of Farming Life, together with a pecuniary legacy.
Resident Property Manager: Vacant.
Senior Ranger/naturalist (based at Crathes): Arthur Martin; tel Crathes (01330) 844651.

OPEN: Garden, Visitor Centre, museum, grounds and other facilities, 1 May to 30 Sep, daily 10-5.30 (last admission 5)

A *Band F: see p 2*

L *Explanatory text in French, German, Italian, Spanish*
⚑ *Upper garden, museum, Visitor Centre, tearoom. Toilet. Wheelchairs available*
Raised map of parterres
🐕 *Dog walk and special car park for visitors with dogs*
◻ 🍴(28) 🪑 ⚘ 📖 **🛈 P**

➡ On A920, 1m W of Pitmedden village and 14m N of Aberdeen. 2m from National Cycle Route 1. Bus: infrequent service passes road end; tel Bluebird Buses, (01224) 212266

Pollok House

POLLOK COUNTRY PARK, 2060 POLLOKSHAWS ROAD, GLASGOW G43 1AT. TEL (0141) 616 6410.

The Maxwell family have lived here since the mid-13th century. Three earlier castles were replaced by the present house (c1740) after consultation with William Adam. The house was extended in 1890 by Sir John Stirling Maxwell, and now contains an internationally famed collection of paintings as well as porcelain and furnishings appropriate to a country house of the Edwardian period. It is set within Pollok Country Park, also home of The Burrell Collection.

Sir John Maxwell placed the 1,118-acre estate under the protection of the first Conservation Agreement of the Trust, of which he was a founder member. The house was gifted to the City of Glasgow in 1966 by Mrs Anne Maxwell Macdonald. The Trust was invited to manage the house in partnership with Glasgow City Council from 1 May 1998; the Gardens, Country Park and The Burrell Collection continue to be managed by the City Council.

Property Manager: Robert Ferguson.

OPEN: *1 Apr to 31 Oct, daily 10-5; 1 Nov to 31 Mar, daily 11-4 (closed 25/26 Dec and 1/2 Jan). Gardens, Country Park and Burrell Collection open all year (details on 0141 649 7151).*

A *Band H: see p 2; free, 1 Nov to 31 Mar*

L *Explanatory text in French, German, Italian and Spanish*

♿ *Shop, restaurant and servants' quarters*

☺ ✕ *(60 plus additional 50 by arrangement)*

 P **E**

➡️ **Off M77 junction 1, follow signs for Burrell Collection, 3m S of Glasgow city centre. On National Cycle Routes 7 & 75. Frequent bus and rail (Pollokshaws West station) from Glasgow city centre; tel (0141) 332 7133.**

Preston Mill & Phantassie Doocot

EAST LINTON, EAST LOTHIAN, EH40 3DS. TEL EAST LINTON (01620) 860426.

OPEN: *Good Friday to Easter Monday and 1 May to 3 Oct, Mon-Sat 11-1 and 2-5, Sun 1.30-5; weekends in Oct, 1.30-4 (last admission 20 mins before closing, morning and afternoon)*

A *Band K: see p 2*

L *Explanatory text in Dutch, French, German, Italian, Japanese, Spanish*

♿ *Ground floor, shop, grounds. Toilet*

➡️ **Off A1, in East Linton, 23m E of Edinburgh. Bus: Lowland SMT (No 106) from Edinburgh to East Linton; tel (0131) 663 9233**

Since the 16th century there has been a mill on this site and the present stone buildings date from the 18th century. The conical roofed kiln and attractive red pantiled buildings make Preston Mill a popular haunt for photographers and artists, while the nearby millpond with resident ducks and geese provides the finishing touches to an idyllic countryside spot. The water-wheel and the grain milling machinery it powers are relatively modern and the mill was still used commercially until 1959. Visitors can see and hear the mechanisms in action and find out about the working life of a miller. There is also an exhibition on milling.

Given by the Trustees of the late Mr John Gray in 1950 and restored by public appeal; machinery renovated by Messrs Ranks Hovis McDougall plc.

Phantassie Doocot, a short walk away, once held 500 birds. Obtain key from the Mill.

Given in 1962 by Mr William Hamilton of Phantassie Farm.

Resident Property Manager: Karen Caldwell.

Priorwood Garden & Dried Flower Shop

MELROSE, BORDERS, TD6 9PX.
TEL MELROSE (01896) 822493.
SHOP: TEL MELROSE (01896) 822965.

OPEN: 1 Apr (or Good Friday if earlier) to 30 Sep, Mon-Sat 10-5.30, Sun 1.30-5.30; 1 Oct to 24 Dec, Mon-Sat 10-4, Sun 1.30-4

A *Band N: see p 2*

♿ *Ramp to garden and dried flower shop*

🛍 *Trust gift shop, 9 Jan to 31 Mar, Mon-Sat 12-4; 1 Apr to 24 Dec, Mon-Sat 10-5.30, Sun 1.30-5.30.*

→ **Off A6091, in Melrose, adjacent to Abbey. Bus: Lowland SMT (No 62) from Edinburgh and Peebles to Melrose; tel (0131) 663 9233**

A unique garden where most of the plants grown are suitable for drying. With the help of volunteers, Priorwood markets a wide variety of dried flower arrangements through its own dried flower shop. Visitors can enjoy a stroll through the adjacent orchard, which includes many varieties of historic apple trees. Priorwood Garden is overlooked by Melrose Abbey and is a short walk from Harmony Garden (see separate entry). Day courses on flower drying throughout the year: contact property for details.

Purchased in 1974.

Property Manager: Catherine Ross.

Rockcliffe

DUMFRIES & GALLOWAY.

The Trust owns several properties in this area. Programme of guided walks in summer. **Mote of Mark**, 20-acre site of an ancient hill-fort, and **Rough Island**, 20-acre bird sanctuary. Owing to the sensitivity of ground-nesting birds, the public are requested not to visit the island during May and June.

Given by Messrs John and James McLellan in 1937 in memory of their brother, the late Col William McLellan, CBE, of Orchard Knowes.

Muckle Lands and Jubilee Path, 51½ acres of rough coastline between Rockcliffe and Kippford.

Given by Miss Hilda G Longworth of Greywalls, Rockcliffe, in 1965.

Auchenvhin, Rockcliffe village: house and contents, two cottages and seven acres. Not open to the public.

Bequeathed to the Trust in 1969 with an endowment by Major J I A McDiarmid.

In October 1971 Mrs M E McLellan of Glenluffin, Rockcliffe, presented 9½ acres of coastline near the Merse, Rockcliffe. In September 1990 Mrs M Anderson of Waterfoot, Rockcliffe, presented 1 acre of coastline near the Merse.

**Property Manager: Trevor Jones, Threave House, Castle Douglas, DG7 1RX.
Tel Castle Douglas (01556) 502575.
Ranger/naturalist: Judy Baxter;
tel Castle Douglas (01556) 630262.**

OPEN: *All year*

   Toilet at Rockcliffe

🚶 **R** **P** ☀

➡ **Off A710, 7m S of Dalbeattie**

St Abb's Head

National Nature Reserve

**RANGER'S COTTAGE, NORTHFIELD, ST ABBS, EYEMOUTH, BORDERS, TD14 5QF.
TEL COLDINGHAM (018907) 71443,
FAX (018907) 71606.**

The sheer 300-ft high cliffs between farmland and the North Sea are pounded by the sea below, but higher up are home to colonies of guillemots, kittiwakes, razorbills, shags, fulmars, puffins and herring gulls which nest on narrow ledges from April to August. St Abb's Head was declared a National Nature Reserve in 1983 and is the most important location for cliff-nesting seabirds in south-east Scotland. The offshore waters are part of Scotland's first voluntary marine nature reserve, which was declared in 1984. Exhibition, toilets.

Purchased in 1980 with the aid of special funds – a legacy for the encouragement of bird-life and the Trust's own Coastline and Islands Fund – and generous grant-aid from the Countryside Commission for Scotland. Co-finance from the European Agricultural Guidance and Guarantee Fund in 1998 is enabling the upgrading of the interpretation of this National Nature Reserve.

OPEN: *Nature Reserve and toilets, all year. Nature Reserve Centre, 1 Apr (or Good Friday if earlier) to 31 Oct, daily 10-5) (parties by arrangement only)*

A *Nature Reserve Centre, Band N: see p 2*

   Toilet. Free parking. Access by car to lighthouse.

🐕 *Dogs must be kept on leash*

🐾 *(not NTS)*

📷 **R**

P *Please use car park beside Nature Reserve Centre at Northfield Farm steading: no vehicles on road to lighthouse except those carrying disabled, elderly or infirm visitors. Parking £1.*

☀

➡ **Off A1107, 2m N of Coldingham**

Lumsdaine Farm coastal strip. 167 acres of cliff and foreshore donated to the Trust by the Pearl Assurance Company Ltd in 1984. Part of the same Grade 1 Site of Special Scientific Interest as St Abb's Head.

Blackpotts grazing block. 123 acres purchased in 1994 to alleviate grazing pressure on the clifftop during summer.

Ranger/naturalist: Kevin Rideout.

St Kilda

*National Nature
Reserve*

WESTERN ISLES.

Remote and spectacular,
the St Kilda archipelago lies
41 miles west of Benbecula.
Its main island of Hirta
maintained its population
until 1930, when the
islanders were evacuated
at their own request.
Fowling among the great
colonies of sea-birds
(puffins for feathers and
meat, young fulmars for

OPEN: *All year*

oil and young gannets for meat) was the main employment, augmented by sheep herding,
crofting and fishing. Each year, Trust working parties conserve and repair buildings, as well as
carrying out archaeological work. Details on the work parties are available from NTS Argyll,
Lochaber & the Western Isles Regional Office: see below.

Bequeathed in 1957 by the 5th Marquess of Bute.

Because of the scientific interest of their natural history, the islands have been leased to Scottish Natural Heritage.

In 1986 St Kilda was designated by UNESCO Scotland's first World Heritage Site.

**No Resident Property Manager. Enquiries to NTS Argyll, Lochaber & the Western Isles Regional Office;
tel Oban (01631) 570000.**

Shieldaig Island

TORRIDON, ROSS-SHIRE.

This 32-acre island is almost
entirely covered in Scots pine
which once formed vast
forests covering much of the
Scottish Highlands.

It was acquired in 1970 with the aid of
the Trust's Coastline and Islands Fund,
which was reimbursed in 1974 by
generous donation from Mr and Mrs
Armistead Peter III of Washington DC
who 'adopted' the island.

**No Resident Property Manager.
Enquiries to Seamus MacNally,
Torridon Mains, Torridon,
Achnasheen, IV22 2EZ;
tel Torridon (01445) 791368,
fax (01445) 791378.**

OPEN: *All year*

➡ **In Loch Torridon, Off Shieldaig, A896**

ROBERT SMAIL'S PRINTING WORKS

7/9 HIGH STREET,
INNERLEITHEN, BORDERS,
EH44 6HA.
TEL INNERLEITHEN (01896)
830206.

Step back in time at this completely restored printing works and see how printing was done at the beginning of this century. The buildings contain an office, paper store with reconstructed water-wheel, composing and press rooms. Visitors can discover the secrets of the printing works from archive-based posters, by watching the printer at work and by trying typesetting by hand. Many historic items and photographs on display also give a fascinating insight into this small Borders town.

Purchased from Cowan Smail in 1986. In 1998 co-finance from the European Regional Development Fund enabled the production of a video recording the vanishing skills used in this unique printing works.

Resident Property Manager: Edward Nicol.

OPEN: Good Friday to Easter Monday and 1 May to 3 Oct, Mon-Sat 10-1 and 2-5, Sun 2-5; weekends in Oct, Sat 10-1 and 2-5, Sun 2-5 (last admission 45 mins before closing, morning and afternoon)

A *Band I: see p 2*

♿ *Shop, office*

➔ **30m S of Edinburgh. Bus: Lowland SMT (No 62) from Edinburgh or Peebles; tel (0131) 663 9233**

SOUTER JOHNNIE'S COTTAGE

MAIN ROAD, KIRKOSWALD, SOUTH AYRSHIRE, KA19 8HY.
TEL KIRKOSWALD (01655) 760603.

OPEN: Good Friday to 3 Oct, daily 11.30-5; weekends in Oct, 11.30-5 (last admission 4.30)

A *Band K: see p 2*

L *Explanatory text in Dutch, French, German, Italian*

P *Car park at S end of village*

➔ **On A77, in Kirkoswald, 4m SW of Maybole. 4m from National Cycle Route 7. Bus: hourly service Ayr-Girvan; tel (0141) 332 7133**

The home of John Davidson, village souter (shoemaker), who was the original Souter Johnnie of Robert Burns' *Tam o' Shanter*. Life-sized stone figures of the Souter, Tam, the innkeeper and his wife are in the restored ale-house in the cottage garden. The thatched cottage, recently refurbished, contains period furniture, Burns relics and a reconstructed souter's workshop.

The Trust took over the cottage in 1932 from the local committee which had restored it.

Property Manager: Jan Gibson; tel (home) (01655) 760671.

Staffa

W of Mull, Argyll & Bute.

This uninhabited island, only half-a-mile long by quarter-of-a-mile wide, is famous for its basaltic formations, distinctive stepped columns created when the lava of volcanic eruptions cooled many millions of years ago. These columns form the cathedral-like stature of Fingal's Cave, immortalised by Mendelssohn in his celebrated *Hebrides* overture. Other famous visitors to the island have included Queen Victoria and Prince Albert, the artist J M W Turner, and poets and writers Keats, Wordsworth, Tennyson and Sir Walter Scott.

The island was given to the Trust in 1986 by Mr John Elliott, Jr, of New York, as an imaginative way to honour the birthday of his wife Elly. She has been declared Steward of Staffa for her lifetime by the Trust. Donations to the necessarily high cost of improvements to landing facilities may be sent to Trust head office or placed in the donation box near the landing point on the island. Grant aid was given by the Countryside Commission for Scotland, the Highlands and Islands Development Board and the European Regional Development Fund.

No Resident Trust Property Manager. Enquiries to NTS Argyll, Lochaber & the Western Isles Regional Office; tel Oban (01631) 570000.

Open: *All year*

→ 7m W of Mull and 6m NE of Iona. Cruises from Iona, Mull and Oban. See pages 84/85. Landing dependent on suitable weather conditions.

Open: *All year*

→ Off A896, 4½m SW of Lochcarron

Strome Castle

Ross-shire.

The ruined castle is romantically situated on a rocky promontory jutting into Loch Carron, commanding fine views westwards to Skye. First recorded in 1472 when it was a stronghold of the Lords of the Isles, it later belonged to the MacDonnells of Glengarry. Following a quarrel with Kenneth MacKenzie, Lord of Kintail, it fell in 1602 after a long siege and was blown up. The tower remains a heap of rubble but substantial sections of the enclosing wall still stand.

Presented in 1939 by Mr C W Murray of Couldoran.

No Resident Trust Property Manager. Enquiries to Iain Turnbull, Lochalsh House (NTS), Balmacara, Kyle, Ross-shire IV40 8DN; tel (01599) 566325, fax (01599) 566359.

The Tenement House

145 Buccleuch Street, Garnethill, Glasgow G3 6QN. Tel (0141) 333 0183.

OPEN: *1 Mar to 31 Oct, daily 2-5 (last admission 4.30). Weekday morning visits by educational and other groups, by advance booking only*

A Band H: see p 2

L *Explanatory text in French, German*

& *Toilet*

[Braille] *Braille guidebook. Audio tour*

P *Very restricted on-street parking, but within walking distance of city centre*

➜ 3rd left off Rose St or Cambridge St, NW of Sauchiehall St pedestrian shopping area (routes avoiding steep hills). 1m from National Cycle Routes 7 & 75. Cowcaddens underground station, ½m

Glasgow, more than any Scottish city, is associated with tenements. This first-floor flat is a typical late Victorian example, consisting of four rooms and retaining most of its original features such as its bed recesses, kitchen range, coal bunker and bathroom. The furniture, furnishings and personal possessions of Miss Agnes Toward, who lived here for over fifty years, present a fascinating picture of domestic life at the beginning of the 20th century, which is further explained in the ground floor exhibition area.

The first-floor flat was restored by the Trust, after purchasing it in 1982 from the actress Anna Davidson, who had carefully preserved its antique atmosphere after discovering it and buying it seven years earlier. Two flats on the ground floor provide reception, interpretive and educational facilities.

Property Manager: Lorna Hepburn.

Threave Garden & Estate

Castle Douglas, Dumfries & Galloway, DG7 1RX.
Tel Castle Douglas (01556) 502575, fax (01556) 502683.

OPEN: *Estate and garden, all year, daily 9.30-sunset. Walled garden and glasshouses, all year, daily 9.30-5. Visitor Centre and exhibition, 1 Apr (or Good Friday if earlier) to 31 Oct, daily 9.30-5.30.*

A Band D: see p 2

L *Explanatory text in French, German, Italian, Spanish*

& *Most of garden, Visitor Centre, restaurant, shop. Toilet. Wheelchairs and electric battery car available. Reserved places in car park*

[icon] *Induction loop in Visitor Centre*

[dog] *Dog walk*

[icon] *Open as Visitor Centre*

[icon] *(80, plus 40 on terrace) Open dates as Visitor Centre, 10-5*

[icons] R P E

➜ Off A75, 1m W of Castle Douglas. On National Cycle Route 7. Bus: McEwan's (Nos 501/502) from Dumfries to Castle Douglas; tel (0345) 090510

Threave Garden is delightful in all seasons. At 64 acres, it is best known for its spectacular springtime daffodils (nearly 200 varieties), but herbaceous beds are colourful in summer and trees and heather garden are striking in autumn. The Victorian house (not open to the public) is home to the Trust's School of Practical Gardening, offering a one-year postgraduate training course. Guided walks and amateur gardening classes available. Visitor Centre with exhibition. **Threave Estate** provides a good example of integrated management of the land, taking account of agriculture, forestry and nature conservation. Marked walks include a 2.5km estate trail which guides the visitor through this variety of landscapes. The Estate is a wildfowl refuge and the wetland is important for its plants, breeding wading birds and wintering wildfowl. Bird hides provide good cover to enjoy the activity of this wildlife.

The house and estate, 1,196 acres, were given in 1948 by the late Major A F Gordon, DSO, MC, of Threave, with a generous endowment. A further adjoining 301 acres were purchased in 1950 and 1959. Major Gordon left a further substantial bequest enabling the first practical gardening school to be established.

The Visitor Centre, built with grant aid from the Scottish Tourist Board, opened in 1975 and was extended in 1989. A further extension was added in 1995 with co-finance from the European Regional Development Fund and the European Agricultural Guidance and Guarantee Fund. In 1997 the programme of restoration and developement of the Threave House Stables into the Threave Countryside Centre was financed by the Heritage Lottery Fund; Historic Scotland; and Scottish Natural Heritage.

Administrator and Principal of NTS School of Practical Gardening: Trevor Jones, Threave House.
Ranger/naturalist: Bob Elliot; tel Castle Douglas (01556) 502575.

Tighnabruaich Viewpoint

ARGYLL & BUTE.

The indicators, attributed to the Trust and the Scottish Civic Trust, were erected by a Trust supporter in memory of two brothers, who gave generously of their time to the work of the Trust.

OPEN: All year

☀

➡ On A8003, NE of Tighnabruaich

Torridon

TORRIDON MAINS, TORRIDON, ACHNASHEEN, ROSS-SHIRE, IV22 2EZ. TEL TORRIDON (01445) 791368, FAX (01445) 791378.

OPEN: Countryside Centre, 1 May to 30 Sep, Mon-Sat 10-5, Sun 2-5. Estate, Deer Park and Deer Museum (unstaffed), all year, daily

🅰 *Band L: see p 2*

♿ *Ramp into Centre*

➡ N of A896, 9m SW of Kinlochewe. **Bus: Duncan MacLennan, tel (01520) 755239, connects to Strathcarron rail station (20m), daily Jun-Sep, Mon/Wed/Fri Oct-May. Post Bus, tel (01463) 256273 or 256228, connects to Achnasheen rail station (20m), all year Mon-Sat**

A 16,100-acre estate including some of Scotland's finest mountain scenery, comprising Liathach (3,456ft), which has seven tops, and Beinn Alligin (3,232ft). The mountains, in addition to their scenic splendour, hold much of interest to geologists and naturalists. Liathach is of Torridonian sandstone some 750 million years old; the tops, of white quartzite some 150 million years younger. A Trust Countryside Centre, with interpretive display and an audio-visual presentation on wildlife, is at the junction of A896 and the Diabaig road. There is also a Deer Museum located 600 yards on, down the gravel road leading to The Mains.

The original estate (14,100 acres) was accepted by the Commissioners of Inland Revenue in part satisfaction of estate duty ensuing upon the death of the 4th Earl of Lovelace; in May 1967 it was transferred to the care of the Trust through National Land Fund procedures. In 1968 the Trust was presented with a further 2,000 acres at Wester Alligin, immediately to the west of the Torridon estate. The gift, in memory of Sir Charles Blair Gordon, GBE, and Lady Gordon, was made by their sons, Blair, Howard and John Gordon, resident in Canada.

In 1998 the restoration of native woodland was co-financed with National Lottery funds, distributed by the Millennium Commission, through the Millennium Forest of Scotland.

Ranger/Property Manager: Seamus MacNally.

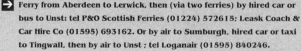
Ferry from Aberdeen to Lerwick, then (via two ferries) by hired car or bus to Unst: tel P&O Scottish Ferries (01224) 572615; Leask Coach & Car Hire Co (01595) 693162. Or by air to Sumburgh, hired car or taxi to Tingwall, then by air to Unst ; tel Loganair (01595) 840246.

Unst

SHETLAND ZE2 9UT

This estate, at the northern tip of Shetland and Britain, extends to 4,707 acres. It comprises ten parcels of land, eight of which are on Unst, and includes a number of houses and agricultural buildings. The smallest parcel is the 30-acre island of Daaey, off Fetlar. Most of the land is in agricultural use and there is a first-class Shetland pony stud. Scenically the three west coast areas of Woodwick, Collaster and Lund are outstanding, with undulating hills, low rocky coastline, beaches, cliffs and voes, all typical of Unst as a whole. The area is of geological, botanical and ornithological importance. There is an interesting wood – the only one on Unst – at Halligarth, containing mostly sycamores.

The estate has been gifted to the NTS but leased back to the donor, Miss Joy Sandison, for her lifetime. Several members of Miss Sandison's family were prominent in the community, including Arthur Edmonston, a surgeon, his brother Laurence, a distinguished naturalist, and nephew Thomas, a botanist. His brother-in-law Henry Saxby wrote *The Birds of Shetland*, published in 1894, eleven years after his death.

No resident Property Manager. Enquiries to NTS Highland Regional Office, tel (01463) 232034.

Venniehill

GATEHOUSE OF FLEET, DUMFRIES & GALLOWAY.

A 3½-acre field with a hilltop viewpoint at the west end of the main street.

Gifted to the Trust by the late Mrs Murray Usher of Cally OBE in 1981.

OPEN: *All year*

➔ Off A75. 1m from National Cycle Route 7

Weaver's Cottage

THE CROSS, KILBARCHAN, RENFREWSHIRE, PA10 2JG. TEL KILBARCHAN (01505) 705588.

OPEN: *Good Friday to 3 Oct, daily 1.30-5.30; weekends in Oct, 1.30-5.30 (last admission 5)*

A *Band K: see p 2*

L *Explanatory text in Spanish*

📺 *Subtitled video*

📖 **E**

➔ M8 Junction 28A, A737, follow signs for Kilbarchan. 12m SW of Glasgow. 1m from National Cycle Routes 7 & 75. Bus: frequent service from Paisley, Glasgow and from Johnstone rail station (2m): tel (0141) 332 7133

This typical 18th-century handloom weaver's cottage houses the last of the 800 looms working in this village in the 1830s. Most Fridays and weekends, the clack, clack of a weaver at work brings this cottage to life again. Locally woven shawls cover the box beds. There is an important display of looms, weaving equipment, domestic utensils, local historical and weaving items. Portraits of former spinners and weavers look at home in the midst of their tools of trade.

Attractive cottage garden. Video programme.

Given in 1954 by the family of the late Miss Christie.

Property Manager: Grace Murray.

West Affric

Open: *All year*

R

P At Kintail or the Forest Enterprise car park near Affric Lodge (OS Map 25 Ref 200 235), reached from Cannich on the A831

The Trust bought this important area in 1993 to protect its wild land character, to restore its natural flora and secure one of the most popular east/west paths in the Highlands. The path, now used only by walkers, was once part of the drove road from Skye to Dingwall.

The 9,050 acres were purchased through a generous legacy and a major grant from the Chris Brasher Trust. West Affric joins the Trust's Kintail and Glomach properties, making a total area of 27,000 acres under Trust care. The restoration of native woodland was co-financed with National Lottery funds, distributed by the Millennium Commission, through the Millennium Forest of Scotland. The Alltbeithe hostel is let to SYHA. The Camban bothy is let to the Mountain Bothies Association. The property is rangered from Kintail.

Enquiries to the Ranger/Property Manager, Kintail: Willie Fraser, Morvich Farm, Inverinate, Kyle IV40 8HQ; tel (01599) 511231, fax (01599) 511417.

ANTONINE WALL

STIRLING.

The Wall was built from the Forth to the Clyde about AD 142 and consisted of ditch, turf rampart and road, with forts every two miles. One of the Trust's sections includes Rough Castle, 3m W of Falkirk, the best preserved of the forts.

Gifted by Kerse Estates, Mr C W Forbes of Callander in 1938.

Under the guardianship of Historic Scotland.

OPEN: *All year*

➔ **Three separate sections along B816, W of Falkirk**

BALNAIN HOUSE

40 HUNTLY STREET, INVERNESS IV3 5HR.
E-MAIL: music@balnain.com WEBSITE: www.balnain.com

Built in 1726 as a merchant's house, Balnain was used as a field hospital for the Hanoverian troops during the battle of Culloden (1746). During the 1880s, it became the base of the Royal Ordnance for survey maps of the Highlands. After 17 years of dedicated restoration work by the Balnain House Trustees, it was opened to the public in April 1993.

It now houses an audio-visual exhibition illustrating Scotland's musical heritage, where visitors are encouraged to try out instruments, including fiddles, clarsachs, guitars and bagpipes, traditional and electronic.

Concerts most nights in summer, ceilidhs every Wed night; informal music sessions and tuition workshops throughout the year. Gift shop with widest range of Celtic music in the Highlands.

Bought by the Trust in 1997. Leased to the Balnain Trust.

Tel Inverness (01463) 715757, fax (01463) 713611.

OPEN: exhibition, 22 May to 30 Jun and 1 to 12 Sep, daily 10-5; 1 Jul to 31 Aug, Mon-Fri 10-8, weekends 10-6; 13 Sep to 21 May, Mon-Sat 10-5. Shop same times, but also midweek 7-9pm (except 1-12 Sep), and Jul/Aug weekdays open till 10pm.

A *Adult £2, concession £1.50, child 50p, family £5: group rates on request*

♿ *Toilet. Restaurant*

🍴 *Reservations for dinner essential: tel (01463) 225585.* **E**

➔ **Inverness town centre, on west bank of River Ness**

CASTLE CAMPBELL

NEAR DOLLAR, CLACKMANNANSHIRE.

In the wooded Dollar Glen stands Castle Campbell. Built in the late 15th century, it was once the home of the chief of Clan Campbell. John Knox is said to have preached here in the 16th century.

Presented to the Trust in 1950 by Mr J E Kerr of Harvieston.

Under the guardianship of Historic Scotland.

OPEN: *1 Apr to 30 Sep, daily 9.30-6.30; 1 Oct to 31 Mar 2000, Mon-Sat 9.30-4.30 (except Thu, pm and Fri, all day), Sun 2-4.30*

A *HS Band 1: see p 2. Free admittance to NTS members*

🏕 📓 **P** *Short walk*

➔ **Off A91, N of Dollar**

Castlehill

DUMBARTON.

4 acres let to West Dunbartonshire Council.

Given to the Trust in 1936 by Captain Angus Cunninghame Graham RN.

OPEN: All year

 On A814

Clava Cairns

NEAR INVERNESS, HIGHLAND.

Dating from around 2000 BC, these circular burial chambers are surrounded by standing stones. The cairns are among the most outstanding Scottish prehistoric monuments. Interpretation boards on site.

Gifted by J G Murray of Culloden in 1945.

Under the guardianship of Historic Scotland.

OPEN: All year

B9006, 5m E of Inverness (near Culloden)

Crookston Castle

GLASGOW.

Early 15th-century tower house on the site of a 12th-century castle. Mary, Queen of Scots, and Darnley stayed here after their marriage in 1565.

Crookston Castle, the Trust's first property, was gifted by Sir John Stirling Maxwell, Bt in 1931.

Under the guardianship of Historic Scotland.

OPEN: Key obtainable from castle cottage at all reasonable times

Brockburn Road, off Crookston Road, 4m SW of city centre. Bus: ½-hourly from Glasgow city centre; tel (0141) 332 7133

Dirleton Castle

EAST LOTHIAN.

Beautiful ruins dating back to 1225, with 14th/16th-century additions. The castle has had an eventful history from its first siege by Edward I in 1298 until its destruction in 1650. The garden encloses a late 16th-century bowling green surrounded by yew trees. Sales kiosk and exhibition.

Gifted in 1981 by Vice-Admiral B C E Brooke.

Under the guardianship of Historic Scotland.

OPEN: 1 Apr to 30 Sep, daily 9.30-6.30; 1 Oct to 31 Mar 2000, Mon-Sat 9.30-4.30, Sun 2-4.30

A HS Band 1: see p 2 (including to Trust members)

On A198, in Dirleton, 3m W of North Berwick

Glenluce Abbey Glebe

Near Glenluce, Dumfries & Galloway.

Part of the glebe adjoining Glenluce Abbey, a ruined Cistercian abbey founded by Rolland, Lord of Galloway, in 1192.

Purchased by the Trust in 1933.

Under the guardianship of Historic Scotland.

OPEN: 1 Apr to 30 Sep, daily 9.30-6.30; 1 Oct to 31 Mar 2000, Sat 9.30-4.30, Sun 2-4.30

A *(Abbey) HS Band 2: see p 2 (including to Trust members)*

➡ **A75, 1½m NW of Glenluce**

Lamb's House

Burgess Street, Edinburgh EH6 6RD.

This residence and warehouse of a prosperous merchant of the late 16th or early 17th century was renovated in the 18th century. The restoration of the exterior was completed in 1979 in association with Edinburgh and Leith Old People's Welfare Council by whom it is used as an old people's day centre.

Presented in 1958 by Lord David Stuart, son of the 4th Marquess of Bute.

OPEN: Visits by prior arrangement only with Lamb's House: tel (0131) 554 3131

➡ **Off A199, in Leith**

Parklea Farm

Inverclyde.

A strip of 68 acres of land on the south bank of the Clyde, leased at a nominal rent to Inverclyde Council as a recreation ground.

Bought from a bequest by Mr Norman P Anderson in 1949.

OPEN: All year

➡ **A8, off M8, 1m E of Port Glasgow**

The Pineapple

N of Airth, Falkirk.

A bizarre structure in the shape of a pineapple, 45ft high, built in 1761 as a garden retreat. The architect is unknown. The policies include a car park, pond and woodland. An orchard of crab-apple trees has been planted in the walled garden.

Given with 16 acres of gardens and policies by the Countess of Perth in 1974. Acceptance made possible by the co-operation of the Landmark Trust, which has leased and restored the building and walls, creating a holiday home. Enquiries for short lets to: Landmark Trust, Shottesbrooke, Maidenhead, Berks. Tel (01628) 825925.

OPEN: Grounds, all year, daily 9.30-sunset

➡ **7m E of Stirling, off A905, then off B9124**

Preston Tower

Prestonpans, East Lothian.

Adjacent to Hamilton House, Preston Tower was built by the Hamilton family in the 15th century; burned by Cromwell in 1650, then rebuilt with Renaissance addition on top. Also, 17th-century doocot and wall.

Purchased by the Trust in 1969.

Under the guardianship of East Lothian Council. No dogs in gardens (except guide dogs).

OPEN: *All year*

🅿

➡ Off A198, 8½m E of Edinburgh

Provan Hall

Auchinlea Road, Easterhouse, Glasgow G34 9QN.

Built in the 15th century, this is probably the most perfect pre-Reformation mansion house in Scotland.

Given to the Trust in 1938. Now part of Auchinlea Park, the property is managed by Glasgow City Council.

Custodian: Steven Allan; tel (0141) 771 4399.

OPEN: *All year, Mon-Fri 9-4.30 (except 25/26 Dec and 1/2 Jan and when special events are in progress)*

➡ B806, N of M8, 3m from city centre

Provost Ross's House

(*Aberdeen Maritime Museum*)
Shiprow, Aberdeen AB1 2BY.

Built in 1593, Provost Ross's House is the third oldest house in Aberdeen. In 1952, when in danger of demolition, the house was acquired from the Town Council, together with a substantial donation. It now houses part of the new Aberdeen Maritime Museum, operated by the City of Aberdeen Council, which gives a wonderful insight into the rich maritime history of the city.

OPEN: *Maritime Museum, all year, Mon-Sat 10-5, Sun 11-5*

Scotstarvit Tower

Cupar, Fife KY15 5PB.

Situated three-quarters of a mile west of Hill of Tarvit Mansionhouse, this fine tower was known to have existed in 1579.

Gifted, together with neighbouring Hill of Tarvit, by Miss E C Sharp in 1949.

Under the guardianship of Historic Scotland.

OPEN: *Good Friday to Easter Monday and 1 May to 30 Sep, daily 1.30-5.30; weekends in Oct, 1.30-5.30 (key at Mansionhouse)*

🅿 *Short walk*

➡ Off A916, 2½m S of Cupar

Threave Castle

Castle Douglas, Dumfries & Galloway.

This 14th-century Douglas stronghold stands on Threave Island in the River Dee.

Gifted in 1948, together with neighbouring Threave House and garden, by Major A F Gordon DSO, MC.

Under the guardianship of Historic Scotland.

OPEN: 1 Apr to 30 Sep, daily 9.30-6.30. Closed in winter

A *HS Band 2: see p 2 (including to Trust members) (includes ferry)*

♿ *Toilet at car park. Access to castle by boat service only. Not recommended for physically disabled persons.*

📷 **P**

➡ **Off A75, 1m W of Castle Douglas**

PROPERTIES OWNED BY THE NATIONAL TRUST FOR SCOTLAND BUT NOT OPEN TO THE PUBLIC

Abertarff House

Church Street, Inverness, IV1 1EU.

Dating from the 16th century and one of the oldest houses in the burgh, Abertarff was presented by the National Commercial Bank of Scotland to the Trust in 1963. Its restoration, completed in 1966, was marked by a Civic Trust Award. It is now the Trust's Highland Regional Office.

Not open to visitors

Beaton's Croft House

40 Bornesketaig, Kilmuir, Isle of Skye, IV51 9YS

Acquired in 1997, Beaton's Croft House is a late 18th-century traditional Skye thatched house situated in the crofting township of Bornesketaig at the north end of Skye. The cottage is managed as self-catering accommodation and is therefore not open to the public to protect the privacy of paying tenants.

Not open to visitors. Special visits can occasionally be arranged: tel Iain Turnbull (01599) 566325. For holiday bookings, tel Holidays Department at Trust head offece.

Calanais Blackhouse

Lewis, Western Isles.

Blackhouse dating from 1760 to 1800. Development under consideration.

Acquired by the Trust in 1934.

Not open to visitors

Charlotte Square

EDINBURGH.

Charlotte Square, designed by Robert Adam in 1791, is considered one of his masterpieces of urban architecture. In addition to No 7 (see The Georgian House, page 31), the Trust owns Nos 5 and 6 on the north side and Nos 26-31 on the south side.

Nos 5, 6 and 7 Charlotte Square and certain chattels were accepted by the Commissioners of Inland Revenue in part satisfaction of estate duty arising from the death of the 5th Marquess of Bute. The property was conveyed to the Trust through National Land Fund procedures in 1966. The Trust thus became the owner of No 5, its headquarter offices, which it had occupied as tenant since 1949. No 6 is leased by the Trust to the Bute House Trust. It has been renamed Bute House and the Trustees have adapted it to serve as the official residence of the Secretary of State for Scotland.

In April 1996 the Trust purchased Nos 26-31, with generous help from the Heritage Lottery Fund and the Secretary of State for Scotland. They are being repaired for use primarily as the Trust's head office, with public gallery and exhibition space.

Not open to visitors at present

Hamilton House

PRESTONPANS, EAST LOTHIAN.

Built 1628 by John Hamilton, a prosperous Edinburgh burgess.

Bought and restored by the Trust in 1937.

House is let and open only by prior arrangement with NTS Lothians, Borders, Dumfries & Galloway Regional Office; tel (01721) 722502

➡ **Off A198, 8½m E of Edinburgh**

Kippen Smiddy

IN KIPPEN, STIRLING

Typical rural, early 18th-century blacksmith's shop forming part of a dwelling-house occupied by the same family of smiths from 1721 until 1986. Contains many authentic tools and artifacts.

Gifted in 1982 by Mr Andrew Rennie.

May open to public by prior arrangement and on advertised 'open' days. For information contact NTS Central, Tayside & Fife Regional Office, tel Perth (01738) 631296

➡ **Off A811, 10m W of Stirling**

Linlithgow Houses

44-48 HIGH STREET, LINLITHGOW, WEST LOTHIAN.

Two typical 16th- or 17th-century houses, restored in 1958 and let.

Given by the late Mr J G B Henderson in 1938.

Not open to visitors

➡ **Off M9**

Newhailes House

Musselburgh, East Lothian.

Built by architect James Smith in 1686, and bought in 1707 by Sir David Dalrymple, who enlarged and developed the house. Newhailes became a centre of the Scottish Enlightenment and played host to many famous figures of the time.

House and stable block undergoing major restoration and not open to the public. Access to Newhailes Plant Centre freely available.

Not open to visitors

→ **Off Newhailes Road (A6095)**

House and policies donated by the Trustees of the late Sir C M Dalrymple.

Acquired in 1997 with generous grant aid from the Heritage Lottery Fund, the National Art Collections Fund and the Secretary of State for Scotland, on advice from the Historic Buildings Council, Scotland, and by public appeal. A programme of restoration, conservation and presentation of the property to the public was begun in 1998 with co-finance from the European Regional Development Fund and Historic Scotland, whilst the associated Conservation Plan has been part-funded by the Heritage Lottery Fund.

For information contact the Estate Office, tel (0131) 665 2869

Northgate House

32 Northgate, Peebles, Borders.

A 'B'-listed stone house built around 1840, now converted into offices for the Trust's Lothians, Borders, Dumfries & Galloway Region.

Purchased in 1996.

Not open to visitors

The Old Granary

West Mill Street, Perth.

Dating from the late 18th century, the Old Granary has been restored by the Trust's Little Houses Improvement Scheme. Six flats for senior citizens were created on the upper floors, and are now in private ownership.

The building also provides offices and a meeting room for the Trust's Central, Tayside & Fife Region.

The restoration was made possible in 1988 by the generous assistance of the Christina Mary Eckford and the Gannochy Trusts; the Scottish Development Agency; the Historic Buildings Council for Scotland and Perth and Kinross District Council.

Not open to visitors

The Old Schoolhouse

Cottown, Perth & Kinross.

A unique, clay-built, thatched-roof cottage dating from 1745, purchased by the Trust in 1993.

The property's acquisition and restoration is funded by the National Heritage Memorial Fund, Perth & Kinross Heritage Trust and Historic Scotland. Detailed technical advice is also being provided by Historic Scotland. Future management and opening of the Schoolhouse is under consideration and an announcement will be made in *Heritage Scotland* in due course.

For information contact NTS Central, Tayside & Fife Regional Office, tel Perth (01738) 631296

Plewlands House

South Queensferry, near Edinburgh.

Built in 1643, the house is of the L-plan design with the stair unusually placed half-way along the side of the north wing. It has been restored to modern standards to provide private housing.

Gifted by Miss Irene Ferguson in 1953.
Not open to visitors

 On B924

Sailor's Walk

Kirkcaldy, Fife.

17th-century group of merchants' houses restored in 1950, gaining a Civic Trust Award.

Given in 1950 by Kirkcaldy Burgh Council.
Not open to visitors

On A92 in town centre

Stenhouse Mansion

Stenhouse Mill Lane, Edinburgh.

This was the home of Patrick Ellis, Edinburgh merchant, in the early 17th century; the date 1623 is above the doorway. Adapted by the Trust and let to the Secretary of State for the Environment as a conservation centre.

Given by the Greyhound Racing Association in 1938.
Not open to visitors

Turret House

Abbey Court, Kelso, Borders, TD5 7JA.

A dominant feature of Abbey Court, opposite Kelso Abbey.

Acquired in 1965.
Not open to visitors

Just off A698

Wester Kittochside Farm

East Kilbride, South Lanarkshire.

A traditional small 100-acre farm typical of north Lanarkshire with Georgian farmhouse and contents, tools and farm implements, dating from the period of transition from horse-powered to mechanised agriculture. The creation of The Museum of Scottish Country Life, on additional land purchased in 1997, has been made possible with generous co-finance from the Heritage Lottery Fund, the European Regional Development Fund, the Lanarkshire Development Agency and Historic Scotland. The Museum, incorporating the traditional farm, will be managed by the National Museums of Scotland in partnership with the Trust, and is expected to open in 2001.

Gifted in 1992 by Mrs M S C Reid.

Not open to visitors

OTHER PLACES OF INTEREST TO VISIT
(properties with which the Trust has been closely connected)

Achamore Gardens
Isle of Gigha, Argyll & Bute.

In 1962 the late Lt-Col Sir James Horlick, Bt, Achamore House, presented to the Trust his collection of valuable plants, including rhododendron hybrids, along with an endowment which formed the Horlick Gardens Fund. Many of the plants are being established in the Trust's own gardens – notably at Brodick Castle. Garden open all year, daily, by courtesy of the owner, Mr Derek Holt of Holt Leisure Parks. Ferries from Tayinloan, Kintyre, 1 mile from pier. Publication. Tel Gigha (01583) 505254.

ADMISSION: ADULTS £2. CHILDREN AND SENIOR CITIZENS £1.

Auchindrain Township Open Air Museum
On A83, 6m SW of Inveraray, Argyll & Bute.

An original communal-tenancy farming township, dating from the 15th century. Restored houses and barns furnished in the style of the 19th century. Visitor Centre, shop, car park. Open: Apr to Sep, daily 10-5. Tel Furnace (01499) 500235.

ADMISSION: ADULTS £3. CHILDREN £1.50, SENIOR CITIZENS £2.50, FAMILY £8.

Cammo
Off A90, Cramond Brig, Edinburgh.
The estate of Cammo (94 acres) was bequeathed to the Trust by Mr Percival Louis Maitland-Tennent. The property is now feued to the City of Edinburgh Council for public open space and is subject to a Conservation Agreement.

Crail Museum and Heritage Centre
62-64 Marketgate, Crail, Fife.
Established by the Crail Preservation Society and now run by Crail Museum Trust. Open: Easter week and Jun to end Sep, Mon-Sat 10-1 and 2-5, Sun 2-5. Remainder Apr, all May, Sat/Sun and public holidays, 2-5. Tel Crail (01333) 450869.

ADMISSION FREE.

Crarae Gardens
On A83, 10m S of Inveraray, nr Minard, Argyll & Bute.

A woodland garden in a most picturesque setting on the west side of Loch Fyne. The garden contains many remarkable plants with azaleas, rhododendrons and eucalyptus a speciality. National Collection of *Nothofagus*. Part of the new Forest Garden, a protected environment for the natural regeneration of habitats and species, will officially open this year. Open: all year, daily; Apr to Oct 9-6, winter during daylight hours. Tel Minard (01546) 886614/ 886388. E-mail: info@crarae-gardens.org Website: www.crarae-gardens.org

ADMISSION: ADULTS £2.50, CHILDREN £1.50, FAMILY £7.

Fife Folk Museum
The Weigh House, Ceres, Fife.
The Fife Folk Museum is a registered independent museum administered by the Fife Folk-Museum Trust. The collection, which is entirely donated, illustrates the economic and cultural history of Fife and includes an outdoor display of agricultural implements. A Heritage Trail, open all year, starts in the car park below the Museum. Open: 2 to 11 Apr and 15 May to 10 Oct, daily, 2-5. Tel Ceres (01334) 828180 (messages only).

ADMISSION: ADULTS £2.50, CHILDREN 50P, SENIOR CITIZENS £2 AND PRE-BOOKED ADULT PARTIES £1.50.

John Knox House
43-45 High Street, Edinburgh.
A 15th-century timber-framed town house associated with John Knox and James Mossman, goldsmith to Mary, Queen of Scots. Open: all year (except 25/26 Dec, 1/2 Jan), Mon-Sat 10-5 (last entry 4.30). Tel (0131) 556 2647.

ADMISSION: ADULTS £1.95, CHILDREN 75P (UNDER 7 FREE), CONCESSIONS £1.50.

McDouall Stuart Museum
Rectory Lane, Dysart, Fife.
This building was the birthplace of John McDouall Stuart, the famous Australian explorer. Open: 1 Jun to 31 Aug, daily 2-5 (other times by appointment). For information tel Kirkcaldy (01592) 412860.

ADMISSION FREE.

Scottish Fisheries Museum
Anstruther Harbour, Fife.
Open: 1 Apr to 31 Oct, Mon-Sat 10-5.30, Sun 11-5; 1 Nov to 31 Mar, Mon-Sat 10-4.30, Sun 2-4.30 (closed 25/26 Dec and 1/2 Jan). Wheelchair friendly. Tel Anstruther (01333) 310628.

ADMISSION: ADULTS £3.50, CHILDREN (UNDER 16) AND SENIOR CITIZENS £2.50, FAMILY TICKET £10. PRE-BOOKED PARTIES, ADULTS £3.20, CONCESSIONS £2.20, SCHOOLS £2.50. ACCOMPANYING ADULT FREE.

St Andrews Preservation Trust Museum and Garden
12 North Street, St Andrews.
This charming 16-century building houses a wealth of material covering many aspects of St Andrews' colourful history. The newly opened garden is one of the hidden delights of the town. Open Easter weekend, 22 May to 2 Oct and St Andrew's Week, daily 2-5. Tel (01334) 477629.

ADMISSION FREE.

Suntrap
Between A8 and A71 in Gogarbank, Edinburgh (near The Gyle).
Exciting 3-acre garden split into many interesting rooms – woodland, Italian, alpine and oriental gardens, water features, peat beds, mixed borders and bedding areas. Here, at the Horticultural Centre of Oatridge Agricultural College, classes in horticulture, landscaping, design and floristry are offered to both the professional and amateur gardener. A gardening advice service is available on Fridays: telephone the garden on (0131) 339 7283 for details. Open: 1 Apr to 30 Sep, daily 9.30-4.30; 1 Oct to 31 Mar, Mon-Fri 9.30-4.30. Groups by appointment.

ADMISSION £1, TRUST MEMBERS FREE.

Viewpoint Indicator
On top of Allermuir Hill, near Hillend on the SW outskirts of Edinburgh.
Gifted to the Trust in 1964 by Mr A W Russell, OBE, WS, the Trust's first Secretary and Treasurer when it was formed in 1931. Restored in 1991 by his son George Russell.

Little Houses Improvement Scheme (LHIS)
Over 200 private houses restored in a manner approved by the Trust and protected by NTS Conservation Agreements. Found all over Scotland, from Inverness to the Borders, all denoted by a plaque. Many located in Fife burghs — Pittenweem, St Monans, Crail, Anstruther, Dysart and Falkland. Not in Trust ownership and not open to the public.

Opening times and admission charges correct at time of going to press.

SELF-CATERING HOLIDAYS

The Trust currently has 34 properties available for self-catering holidays, situated in or around some of the most splendid castles, mansion houses and gardens, or in beautiful countryside. The choice varies from a traditional thatched cottage for two on the Isle of Skye (above) to a luxury apartment at Mar Lodge sleeping up to 15 people. All our properties are comfortably furnished in a manner reflecting their character, and priced according to their situation, style and capacity.

Members of The National Trust for Scotland will receive a 5 per cent discount on any booking made and non-members making a booking will receive a Touring Pass allowing them to visit local Trust properties free of charge during their holiday. For full details please contact: Holidays Department, The National Trust for Scotland, 5 Charlotte Square, Edinburgh EH2 4DU; tel (0131) 243 9331, fax (0131) 243 9302, e-mail lmackay@nts.org.uk

Beechgrove Cottage, Pitmedden

CRUISES

The Trust has organised an exciting programme of holidays for 1999. Our annual cruise aboard the *Black Prince*, which leaves Leith on 3 June and returns there on 17 June, will be visiting the Islands of the North. Hoy, Fair Isle, Skye, Iceland and the Westmann Islands. The Faroes and Unst will be our destinations and we will be accompanied by a team of expert lecturers and professional entertainers.

We are also offering an exciting new cruise in the Aegean with Swan Hellenic, aboard *Minerva*, which will visit Delphi, circumnavigate Mount Athos, transit the Corinth Canal and spend two days in Istanbul.

We have an allocation of cabins on the famous *Hurtigruten* or Norwegian post boat, which will take passengers to the small, otherwise inaccessible ports on Norway's spectacular coastline. The River Danube, which connects eight countries – from the Black Forest to the Black Sea – is Europe's second longest river. Our exciting cruise will sail from Vienna in Austria all the way to Constanta in Romania.

For details of these exciting holidays, please contact: Holidays Department, The National Trust for Scotland, 5 Charlotte Square, Edinburgh EH2 4DU; tel (0131) 243 9333/4, fax (0131) 243 9302, e-mail lmackay@nts.org.uk

BASE CAMPS

The Trust offers economical accommodation for groups at two of its properties.

Shore Lodge, Brodick

Situated within the grounds of Brodick Castle on the Isle of Arran, this newly completed centre will be available for let from early 1999. It has dormitory-style accommodation for 12, and separate leaders' rooms. For details, contact Brodick Castle Administrator; tel (01770) 302202, fax (01770) 302312.

House of Dun Base Camp

On the House of Dun estate, off the A935 Brechin to Montrose road, a former estate house has been converted and equipped to provide basic but comfortable accommodation for up to 14 people.

The house comprises two bunk-bedded rooms and one twin-bedded room, with kitchen, toilets and showers. Open all year (except first two weeks in February): for details, contact the House of Dun Property Manager, tel (01674) 810264; fax (01674) 810722.

Kintail Outdoor Centre

The centre is situated 16 miles from Kyle of Lochalsh. It is on the banks of the River Croe, in an area of lochs and mountains offering a wide variety of outdoor pursuits. Countryside Rangers are on hand to help visiting groups make the most of their stay.

Up to 28 can be accommodated in four dormitories and two leaders' rooms, and kitchen, toilets and showers are provided. For details, contact Willie Fraser, Kintail Property Manager, tel (01599) 511231, fax (01599) 511417.

Mol Mor, Torridon

Mol Mor, part of a converted farm steading at the head of Loch Torridon, provides good quality basic accommodation for up to ten people. The three rooms – two four-bedded and one two-bedded – are fitted with bunk beds. The kitchen is well equipped and there are also showers, a laundry and central heating. For details, contact Seamus MacNally, Torridon Property Manager, tel (01445) 791368; fax (01445) 791378.

CARAVANNING AND CAMPING

The Trust has caravanning and camping facilities at three of its properties.

Culzean Country Park Camping and Caravanning Site

Glenside, Culzean, South Ayrshire, KA19 8JK.

Site leased to the Camping and Caravanning Club Ltd. Tel: Kirkoswald (01655) 760627.

Facilities include toilets (including disabled facility), chemical toilet emptying point, wash basins, showers, laundry facilities, electrical hook-ups, payphone and children's play area.

Open dates: 22 March to 1 November: 90 pitches.

Nearby Trust properties to visit:
Bachelors' Club, Tarbolton; Brodick Castle, Isle of Arran; Broughton House, Kirkcudbright; Culzean Castle & Country Park; Greenbank Garden, Holmwood House, Hutchesons' Hall, Pollok House, The Tenement House (all in Glasgow); Souter Johnnie's Cottage, Kirkoswald; Threave Garden, Castle Douglas and Weaver's Cottage, Kilbarchan.

Morvich Caravan Club Site

Inverinate, Lochalsh, Highland IV40 8HQ.

Site on banks of River Croe near Loch Duich, leased to The Caravan Club. Tel (summer only): Glenshiel (01599) 511354.

Facilities include: toilets (including for the disabled), laundry and drying room, TV, gas and electric points, dishwashing, family games room, mother and baby room, hard standings. Waste points for motor caravans. Salmon and sea trout fishing available.

Open dates: 26 March to 25 October: 106 pitches (tent campers also accepted).

Nearby Trust properties to visit:
Balmacara Estate, Corrieshalloch Gorge, Falls of Glomach, Inverewe Garden and Kintail and Morvich.

The National Trust for Scotland Caravan and Camping Site. Glencoe

Glencoe, Highland PA39 4LA.

Site leased to Bill McCubbin. Tel: Glencoe (01855) 811397 (summer) or (01855) 811278 (winter). Facilities include toilets (including disabled facilities), showers, chemical disposal point, cooking shelters, dishwashing facilities, laundry room with token-operated washing and drying machines, electric hook-ups, payphone and shop.

Open dates: 1 April to 31 October: 100 pitches.

The Trust has over 30 Members' Centres and Friends' groups throughout Scotland, and one in London. These allow members to share interests and find out more about the Trust through a diverse programme of talks, social events and day outings. Some offer weekend tours in Scotland and even holidays abroad. Members' Centres provide vital help to the Trust in a variety of ways, including fund-raising, recruitment, guiding and practical conservation work. Several run shops which make a significant financial contribution. During the past financial year, Centres raised over £80,000. Enquiries about joining should be made directly to the appropriate secretary listed below.

SECRETARIES, MEMBERS' CENTRES AND GROUPS

Aberdeen & District Members' Centre Finlay McKichan, 5 Cairnaquheen Gardens, Aberdeen AB2 4HJ: (01224) 315103.

North-East Aberdeenshire Members' Centre Val Fowlie, Balcairn, Old Meldrum, AB51 0EU; (01651) 873227.

West Aberdeenshire & Kincardine Members' Centre Mrs Veronica Hartley, Bogarn, Strachan, Banchory, AB31 6LR: (01330) 850297.

Angus Members' Centre Joyce Cooper, 32 Tailyour Crescent, Montrose, Angus DD10 9BL: (01674) 676783.

Argyll Members' Group Dr Fred Newth, Shona Mhor, Seaview Grazings, Strontian, Acharacle, PH36 4HZ: (01967) 402273.

Ayrshire Members' Centre Miss Myra McLanaghan, Cove, 24 Fenwickland Place, Ayr, KA7 3SL: (01292) 283950.

Banff & Moray Members' Centre Edmund Benzie, 14 Woodlands Crescent, Elgin, Moray IV30 2LY: (01343) 547052.

Bearsden & Milngavie Members' Group Dr Willis Marker, 2 Huntly Drive, Bearsden, Glasgow G61 3LD: (0141) 942 6756.

Borders Members' Group Mrs Lorna Waddell, 163 Roxburgh Street, Kelso, TD5 7DU: (01573) 226570.

Dumfriesshire Members' Group Mrs Shirley Starkey, Underwood Cottage, Steilston, Dumfries DG2 0JJ: (01387) 720839.

Dundee Members' Group Charles Paterson, 11 Barnes Avenue, Dundee DD4 9AE: (01382) 858862.

Eastwood & District Members' Centre Mrs June Watts, 1 Knowes Road, Newton Mearns, Glasgow G77 5PS: (0141) 639 2067.

Edinburgh Members' Centre Miss Tony Ireland, 46 Barnton Court, Edinburgh EH4 6EH: (0131) 339 6629.

East Fife Members' Centre The Hon Mrs A Leslie, Whitefield House, Letham, Cupar KY15 7SB: (01337) 810723.

West Fife Members' Group Mrs Jane Stewart, 23B Main Street, Carnock, Dunfermline KY12 9JG: (01383) 852341.

Galloway Members' Group Ken Inglis, Gelston Mill, Gelston, Castle Douglas DG7 1SH: (01556) 503261.

Glasgow Members' Centre Miss Moira Young, 127 Hatton Gardens, Crookston, Glasgow G52 3PU: (0141) 883 0239.

Highland Members' Centre Miss Linda Bingham, Castlehill House, Inverness IV1 2BA: (01463) 233875.

Inverclyde Members' Centre Fred Reid, 74 Lyle Road, Greenock, PA16 7QT: (01475) 635426.

Lanarkshire Members' Group Chairman: Mrs Marion Dickie, 2 Murchison Drive, East Kilbride, G75 8HF: (013552) 20470.

London Members' Centre Peter Craig, 36 Sherwood Court, Riverside Plaza, Chatfield Road, London SW11 3UY: (0171) 228 5116.

East Lothian Members' Centre Mrs Margaret Russell, 7 Stevenson Park, Longniddry, East Lothian EH32 0PD: (01875) 853370.

Motherwell District Members' Group Mrs Marion Munro, 32 Adele Street, Motherwell ML1 2QF: (01698) 263640.

Perth & Kinross Members' Group Mrs Hilary Young, South Kinrara, Fairmount Terrace, Perth PH2 7AS: (01738) 625343.

Stirling Members' Centre W Jack Sutherland, Daisybank, 7 Back Causeway, Culross, Fife, KY12 8JF: (01383) 881959.

Friends of Alloa Tower Mrs Dorothy Wright, 90 Tullibody Road, Alloa, Clackmannanshire, FK10 2 NL: (01259) 724125.

Friends of Brodick Castle & Country Park Mrs Gail Scott, Ornsay, Lochranza, Isle of Arran KA27 8HJ: (01770) 830304.

Friends of Broughton House & Garden Mrs Dorothy Baron, 35 Fleet Street, Gatehouse of Fleet, DG7 2JT: (01557) 814460.

Friends of Greenbank Mrs Kathy Rice, 23 Langtree Avenue, Glasgow G46 7LJ: (0141) 638 7361.

Friends of Malleny Dr Ian Ogilvie, 11 Cherrytree Gardens, Balerno EH14 5SP: (0131) 449 1960.

Friends of Suntrap Acting Secretary Mrs Margaret Kilpatrick, Borland House, Cleish, Kinross-shire KY13 7LN: (01577) 850218.

Weaver's Cottage Support Group Mrs Patricia Wright, 12 Lexwell Avenue, Elderslie, PA5 9AF: (01505) 324193.

Scotland is renowned for its spectacular and varied scenery and wildlife, and The National Trust for Scotland cares for some 180,000 acres of the most important countryside, which rightly

attracts visitors throughout the year. Early spring, when the snow may be still thick on the ground, is the time to observe displaying golden eagles at Goatfell and Kintail; the clamorous sea-bird colonies of St Abb's Head and the island properties are best enjoyed in May and June; the roaring of the rutting red deer stags reaches a climax in October; the skeins of greylag geese fly into their winter roost in the Wildfowl Refuge at Threave during the darkest months of the winter.

In managing its countryside portfolio, the Trust's fundamental aim might be to keep things just as they are, retaining the wild character that is so attractive: but such 'preservation' often requires active management. A valued pond, home to frogs, toads and dragonflies, will naturally silt up with decaying vegetation; in time it will become marsh, then dryish land and will finally be covered in woodland. In order to retain the pond, and its attendant wildlife, it must be dredged every so often; ponds at Brodie and Crathes have been cleared out in this way by the Trust. Other natural processes include scrub overgrowing

Pond in the grounds of Brodie Castle. Top: red deer stag; centre, dragonfly

Mar Lodge Estate

important grasslands and natural woodland being choked by invasive competitors; the spread of rhododendron into oak woodland at Brodick Country Park is a good example of the latter.

The second part of our countryside conservation is the active restoration of lost or damaged communities of plants and landscape features. The Trust owns many large mountainous properties, all of which are grazed by sheep or deer. Following a major study undertaken by the Trust in 1996-8 with support from the European Union LIFE programme, we have been able to set grazing levels for several important properties including Glencoe and Ben Lawers. Grazing damages young trees and prevents regeneration of woodlands. So the Trust has recently devoted much attention to restoring native woodlands by reducing grazing. At Mar Lodge Estate, a programme of deer culling is underway, allowing regeneration of the internationally important Caledonian pine woods. The Millennium Forest for Scotland has grant-aided many woodland restoration projects. Our programme of mountain footpath repair is also part of the restoration of degraded landscapes.

How is this work achieved? Our ranger/ naturalists are largely responsible for the active management on the ground, but they are dependent on the willing contribution of our Conservation Volunteers. Practical work is underpinned by knowledge gained through survey and monitoring – here, our rangers are helped by the Trust's Nature Conservation Adviser and his contract staff.

Learning with a Trust ranger at Culzean Country Park

The first Trust rangers were appointed in 1969, with funding from the Countryside Commission for Scotland. At first the job was largely interpretive, but later developed into the field of nature and landscape conservation, attracting financial support from the then Nature Conservancy Council. In 1992 CCS and NCC were amalgamated to form Scottish Natural Heritage, which now funds some 200 full-time and 100 seasonal rangers. The National Trust for Scotland, with 27 full-time and 22 seasonal staff, is the largest employer of rangers in Scotland.

The Trust's rangers come from a variety of backgrounds, but all are skilled and practical naturalists, with a strong commitment to conservation. The varied areas in which they work include the mountains of Torridon, the Country Parks at Brodick and Culzean, the woodland properties close to the A9 in east Perthshire and the spectacular coastline at St Abb's Head. They manage our countryside properties sympathetically for wildlife – tree planting, pond improvement and habitat creation are underpinned by wildlife survey and monitoring programmes.

A programme of ranger events is arranged every year – details from the relevant property or Trust Regional Office (addresses on page 4). In the expert company of a ranger, you can enjoy magnificent scenery while learning more about wildlife and land use. Some walks require hillwalking skill , but many others explore low ground and are suitable for everyone. Rangers are also pleased to advise and lead visiting groups, but advance notice of such visits is essential.

In some areas rangers also offer a programme of talks during the summer – details of these are available locally. They also regularly give illustrated talks to interested groups, especially during the winter.

The Trust co-ordinates a year-long Conservation Volunteer programme of working holidays and weekend projects on 40 Trust properties all over Scotland. Up to 800 enthusiastic volunteers complete 112 projects each year. Providing invaluable support to the Trust's property staff and ranger service, the volunteer workforce equates to approximately 15 full-time members of staff. Five local Conservation Volunteer groups (Glasgow, Lothian, Tayside, Grampian and Highland) carry out practical conservation work on weekend projects throughout the year. A wide range of tasks are tackled, including footpath management, scrub clearance, fencing, dyking and tree planting. All projects contribute to the care and protection of Scotland's countryside, wildlife and archaeology. Weekend projects are free: food, accommodation and transport are provided. Between March and November volunteers of all ages and backgrounds, some from as far away as Australia, take part in NTS Thistle Camps, residential working conservation holidays. Projects last from one to three weeks, and are based in breathtaking and often remote locations throughout Scotland. The work is wide-ranging and interesting, offering opportunities

to learn specific skills such as archaeology, species management and footpath repair. Much sought-after are our camps on Fair Isle, Burg, Iona and Mar Lodge Estate. Thistle Camps cost between £35 and £90.

For a 1999 Thistle Camps brochure, please send an sae to: CV Manager, The Countryside Division, The National Trust for Scotland, 5 Charlotte Square, Edinburgh, EH2 4DU or e-mail mhume@nts.org.uk.

Schoolchildren at Gladstone's Land find out about 17th-century Edinburgh

A study box for Preston Mill

Trust properties offer limitless opportunities to all sectors of education. Primary, secondary, tertiary and community groups are all welcome and specific programmes of study may be arranged to match the requirements of visiting students and groups. A developing network of regional education officers will be happy to advise you and help prepare for visits to Trust properties. School parties are always welcome and we encourage teachers and leaders to make use of extensive facilities. We can provide in-service courses either at the property or at an education centre venue, and are happy to host an open afternoon or evening to facilitate the planning of visits. 5-14 curriculum work is particularly well catered for and our staff are keen to help with project- and topic-based learning with many properties offering an educational guide service.

Opportunities exist at our countryside properties for environmental education outdoors and we have our own extensive ranger service. Many of our smaller properties offer the opportunity to study the built environment. Our facilities include costumes, history-based drama activities, spaces for project work and study boxes with objects for handling, which may also be borrowed for use in schools.

Young visitors help to feed a pet lamb at Brodick Country Park

For Standard Grade, Higher and SVQ work enquiries about property details such as architecture, decorative art, paintings, gardens and natural history are welcomed by our department. Students of tourism, ecology and environmental studies may also find our properties a useful resource.

Videos and slides may be borrowed from our library. A range of educational publications – including property-based study packs, special children's guides and leaflets – complement a visit and facilitate further study. Every property has an educational leaflet detailing particular suggestions for study topics.

To encourage educational visits we are able to offer Educational Membership. This not only allows a teacher or lecturer a free preliminary tour before each visit, but thereafter it allows the school, college or group free visits to all properties throughout the year's membership.

Top: Children's collage depicting the 50th anniversary of Leith Hall.
Bottom: With a Trust ranger on the beach at Culzean

School roll up to 50	**£17.00 pa.**
School roll 51-100	**£33.00 pa.**
School roll 101-200	**£40.00 pa.**
School roll 201-500	**£50.00 pa.**
School roll over 500	**£58.00 pa.**
Tertiary Education	**£87.00 pa.**

For further information please contact The Education Department, The National Trust for Scotland, 5 Charlotte Square, Edinburgh EH2 4DU. Tel (0131) 243 9313, fax (0131) 243 9302, e-mail education@nts.org.uk.

Re-enacting the battle of 1314 at Bannockburn

GARDENS IN TRUST

Scotland is internationally renowned for its many fine gardens which flourish in the country's varied climate: from the favoured Inverewe Garden on the shores of Loch Ewe and the developing woodland garden at Balmacara to the sheltered model 17th-century terraced garden at Culross, Scotland's garden heritage is second to none.

The National Trust for Scotland is the country's largest garden owner, with just over 700 acres under intensive cultivation supporting over 13,500 different sorts of plants. The Trust acquired its first garden in 1945 when it accepted Culzean Castle; seven years later Inverewe, Brodick, Falkland Palace and Pitmedden Gardens were added to a developing portfolio which now includes 30 major gardens and designed landscapes and a further 30 smaller gardens. Within this impressive selection, almost every style of Scottish garden history is represented – from the medieval through the 18th-century Picturesque to the 20th-century developments at Falkland Palace, Priorwood and Threave Gardens. Hand-in-hand with the maintenance of historic gardens, the Trust plays an important role in promoting the conservation of the art and craft of practical gardening, not least through its School of Practical Gardening at Threave.

Gardens are forever changing, usually as a result of the natural senescence of their plant components, but also because of changes in fashion in garden design, plant availability and use, and because of pressures of public access. During 1999 significant developments are planned within Trust gardens. These include the remodelling of the walled kitchen garden at Fyvie Castle to display a wide range of Scottish fruit (especially soft fruit) varieties; the initiation of a major refurbishment of the south walled garden at Culzean, including restoration of a large glasshouse range; and the planting of a period kitchen garden at Holmwood. The centenary of the start of Ian Brodie's hybridising of daffodils will be marked by a daffodil show at Brodie Castle on 17-18 April. A historical landscape survey will be developed at House of the Binns; and plant sales will be upgraded at a number of gardens around the country.

If you would like to find out more about the gardens in Trust care, please contact the gardens advisory staff at Trust head office.

Geilston Garden

Each year some 400 Scottish gardens, most of them privately owned, open their gates to the public under the banner of Scotland's Gardens Scheme. Founded in 1931, it is an independent charity and the money raised from garden visitors supports two main beneficiaries – the Queen's Nursing Institute (Scotland) and the gardens fund of The National Trust for Scotland. In addition garden owners may donate up to 40 per cent of their takings to a charity of their choice.

The Scotland's Gardens Scheme handbook, available from any National Trust for Scotland shop at £3 or by post from 5 Charlotte Square, Edinburgh EH2 4DU for £3.75 (including post and packing), lists the gardens open in each region month by month. These gardens include National Trust for Scotland gardens which, though open regularly to the public throughout the year, nominate certain days when their entry money is donated to Scotland's Gardens Scheme.

Crathes Castle garden

On your travels round Scotland, keep an eye open for the distinctive yellow posters of the scheme advertising the local gardens that are open. At all of them you can be assured of a warm welcome. At many of them you will be able to buy plants and enjoy a cup of tea. The garden owners regard it as a compliment to be able to share their garden for a day with the public and you will never be disappointed with your visit.

The National Trust for Scotland is particularly grateful to the garden owners and Scotland's Gardens Scheme for the magnificent financial support they provide each year to help maintain our own gardens. This apart, they contribute so much to the enjoyment of many thousands of visitors to Scotland each year. Please support their efforts by also visiting the local gardens that are open during your travels to Trust properties.

Further information from Scotland's Gardens Scheme, 31 Castle Terrace, Edinburgh EH1 2EL. Tel: (0131) 229 1870; fax:(0131) 229 0443; e-mail: sgsoffice@aol.com.

SCOTLAND'S CHURCHES SCHEME

Scotland's Churches Scheme is fast becoming an established part of Scottish life. This is demonstrated by the number of churches included in its annual handbook, *Churches to Visit in Scotland 1999*, available from major booksellers or from the address below at £3.50, plus £1 for post and packing. The initiative of the Trustees in launching the Scheme four years ago has drawn the attention of a wide public to this remarkable architectural heritage. Many of Scotland's most important buildings are abbeys and churches – not just the great and expansive, but also the small and humble, which are often found in the most beautiful and tranquil of settings. They all represent the rich cultural background of Scotland and the diversity of the nation.

Although not formally included in the Scheme, a number of Trust properties have interesting ecclesiastical associations, with chapels at a number of properties, notably Haddo House, Drum Castle and Falkland Palace.

Further information from Scotland's Churches Scheme, Dunedin, Holehouse Road, Eaglesham, Glasgow G76 0JF. Tel: (01355) 302416.

Here are some remarkable listed properties.

1 **RATE*watch* guarantees competitive interest rates on all our savings accounts until the year 2001.**

2 **Every month we take an average of the rates offered by the Halifax, Abbey National, Nationwide and the Woolwich*. Then we better it.**

3 **With a choice of an Instant Access, 30 Day or 60 Day Savings Account we have a savings account to suit your needs.**

4 **It takes just £50 to open a Royal Bank savings account, or less if you set up a monthly standing order of £20 or more.**

5 **In addition, you can check your balance or transfer funds over the phone 24 hours a day, 365 days a year.**

6 **To find out more you can visit any of our 338 branches across Scotland. Admission is free.**

The Royal Bank
of Scotland

On the 12th day of each month (or nearest business day) until at least January 2001, we will carry out a separate comparison for each of our Instant Access, 30 Day and 60 Day Savings Accounts. We will calculate an average of the rates paid on the comparison accounts specified for each of our accounts, taking the starting points of the advertised tiers for each of our accounts as the comparison point. *The respective comparison accounts used are Halifax (Liquid Gold, Solid Gold and Bonus Gold), Abbey National (Instant Saver, Investor 30 and High Yield Bond), Nationwide (Cash Builder, Capital Builder and Bonus 60) and Woolwich (Prime Gold, Premier 90 and Premier 90). We promise that the rate paid on each tier of our accounts for the next calendar month will be higher than the calculated average rate from the relevant comparison. Our Instant Access Savings Account allows the first ten withdrawals per quarter free, thereafter 50p charge for each withdrawal. 30 Day Savings Account allows one free withdrawal without notice each six month period, thereafter 30 days' notice per withdrawal or if immediate 30 days' interest charge. 60 Day Savings Account allows 60 days' notice per withdrawal or if immediate 60 days' interest charge. Calls may be recorded.

The Royal Bank of Scotland plc. Registered office: 36 St. Andrew Square, Edinburgh EH2 2YB.
Registered in Scotland No. 90312.

THE ROAD TO THE ISLES

The Trust owns a number of Scottish islands as well as having properties or areas of countryside on others. These range from the wild grandeur of St Kilda to the tranquillity of Iona, and from the Goatfell range of mountains on the Isle of Arran to Fingal's Cave on Staffa.

Excellent ferry services exist to carry visitors, and often their cars as well, to a large number of Scottish islands. The major ferry company operating in the Hebrides and the Clyde is Caledonian MacBrayne, with services to 23 islands. The company also operates the mainland ferry links between Gourock and Dunoon and between Tarbert (Loch Fyne) and Portavadie in the Cowal peninsula.

There are also a number of small operators who run daily, weekly or charter cruises to many of the smaller islands. Visitors can enjoy day cruises to the Trust's island of Staffa to visit Fingal's Cave. Sailings to Staffa are operated from Iona, Ulva and Fionnphort, and there are inclusive day tours to Staffa, Iona and Mull from Oban. From Mallaig there is an improved service to the Small Isles — Rum, Eigg, Muck and Canna — which allows day trips to be made by passengers. While the main service to Canna is operated by Caledonian MacBrayne from Mallaig, day trips may also be arranged from Arisaig by Murdo Grant on mv *Shearwater*, or from Mallaig (charter only) on mv *Western Isles* by Bruce Watt.

The Trust's two islands on Loch Lomond, Bucinch and Ceardach, can be viewed from some of the loch excursions operating from Balloch and Luss or the mail boat at Balmaha.

For details about opportunities to visit St Kilda by participating in a work party, contact NTS Argyll, Lochaber & the Western Isles Regional Office; tel Oban (01631) 570000.

Fair Isle, lying between Orkney and Shetland, may be visited by *Good Shepherd IV*, sailing from Grutness, Shetland. Loganair flights from Tingwall, Shetland, may be available: check with the company.

Details about services may be obtained from Tourist Information Centres and the sources listed below.

Most islands in the Firth of Clyde and Western Isles	Caledonian MacBrayne, Ferry Terminal, Gourock PA19 1QP. Tel: (01475) 650100. Website: www.calmac.co.uk
Canna, Rum, Eigg and Muck	Caledonian MacBrayne. Tel: (01475) 650100 or (01687) 462403. Murdo Grant, Arisaig Harbour, Highland (charter only). Tel: (01687) 450224; fax: (01687) 450678. Bruce Watt, Mallaig Harbour, Highland (Rum & Canna only). Tel: (01687) 462233/462320.
Staffa and Iona	Caledonian MacBrayne run day tours to Iona and Staffa from Oban in summer. Tel: (01475) 650100. Gordon Grant Marine Ltd, Achavaich, Isle of Iona. Tel: (01681) 700338 (sailing from Iona and Fionnphort). David B Kirkpatrick, Tigh-na-Traigh, Isle of Iona. Tel: (01681) 700358 (sailing from Iona and Fionnphort, April to October). Iain Morrison ('Turus Mara'), Penmore Mill, Dervaig, Isle of Mull. Tel: (01688) 400242/400297; e-mail turus.mara@dial.pipex.com (sailing from Ulva Ferry, Mull). Esbee Coaches (provide a link between the ferry terminals on Mull at Craignure and Fionnphort). Tel: (01236) 423621, or (01631) 566999 (summer only).
Loch Lomond	Sweeney's Cruises. Tel: (01389) 752376, fax (01389) 721082 (sailing from Balloch). Mullen's Cruises. Tel: (01389) 751481 (sailing from Balloch). Island Cruises. 'Take the High Road Cruise', half-hour sailings (both from Luss during summer). Tel: (01436) 860257. MacFarlane's Mail Boat Cruises. Tel: (01360) 870214 (sailing from Balmaha daily, May to October).
Fair Isle	*Good Shepherd IV*. Tel:(01595) 760222. Loganair. Tel: (01595) 840246.

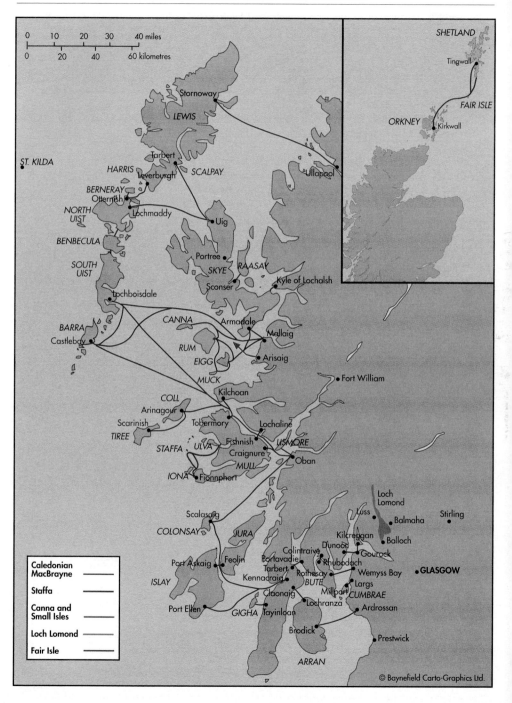

Caledonian MacBrayne ——
Staffa ——
Canna and Small Isles ——
Loch Lomond ——
Fair Isle ——

© Baynefield Carto-Graphics Ltd.

A Gift that's Different

Membership of The National Trust for Scotland makes a wonderful present – it's year-round enjoyment for a friend, relative or colleague.
New members will receive free access to properties in Scotland and those of the National Trust in England, Wales and Northern Ireland and many overseas Trusts. Members also receive our quarterly colour magazine, Heritage Scotland, annual Guide to Scotland's Best and a host of member privileges and benefits. Your Gift of Membership will be presented in an attractive Gift Card needing no extra wrapping. We're looking forward to welcoming your friends and family to The National Trust for Scotland as new members very soon!

Current membership categories and subscription rates – valid until 31 October 1999

☐ Member: £26 per annum
☐ 25 and under: £10 per annum. Please give date of birth __ /__ /__
☐ Family: £42 per annum. Two adults at one address (and any of their children or grandchildren under 18)
☐ Life: £624 (includes guest and cardholder's children under 18)
☐ Life Senior: £335 (age 60 and over; includes guest and cardholder's children under 18)

Over 60s may join at a discount (UK residents):

☐ Senior Member: £17 per annum
☐ Joint Senior: £28 per annum (two adults at one address)

Education, non-profit making societies and corporate commercial rates available on request.

Please note: there are two types of gift membership.

a) A gift for one year. If a donor gives for one year only the subsequent renewal notices and membership card(s) are sent to the recipient(s).

b) A continuing gift. If a donor wishes to continue the gift in future years the subsequent renewal notices and membership card(s) are sent to the donor.

In both cases, all literature is sent to the gift recipient, with the exception of the initial mailing of cards and literature which we usually send to you, the gift donor, to present.
However, if you wish this initial mailing to be sent directly to the gift recipient, please tick this box ☐

To process your gift we must know i) which type and ii) which category of gift yours is to be.

Please tick the appropriate boxes. This gift is to be: a) for one year only ☐   b) a continuing gift ☐

PLEASE PRINT Category of membership required	FOR NTS USE ONLY
	MEMBERSHIP NO.

Donor: Mr/Mrs/Miss/Ms Surname .... Initials ....

Address of donor ....

.... Postcode ....

	TYPE	SOURCE

DAY	MONTH	YEAR

Recipient: Mr/Mrs/Miss/Ms Surname .... Initials ......

Address of recipient ....

.... Postcode ....

Amount received

£

I enclose my remittance (payable to The National Trust for Scotland)/please charge my Credit Card £ ....

Credit Card expiry date: __ / __   Switch Card issue no. or start date: ....

(Visa/Access/American Express/JCB/Mastercard/Switch No. ☐☐☐☐ ☐☐☐☐ ☐☐☐☐ ☐☐☐☐)

I hereby authorise you to debit the above numbered credit card account on an annual basis in respect of this gift renewal until advised by me to the contrary.

When completed, please send to: Membership Services, The National Trust for Scotland, 5 Charlotte Square, Edinburgh EH2 4DU (tel 0131 243 9555, fax 0131 243 9589, e-mail membership@nts.org.uk).

All details held by the Trust in relation to this gift membership are compliant with the Data Protection Act of 1998.

SHARE YOUR ENJOYMENT OF THE PAST IN THE FUTURE

The previous pages illustrate the enormous variety, beauty and interest of Trust properties acquired and cared for thanks to the generosity of supporters over the last 68 years. The proper maintenance of over 100 properties occupying around 185,000 acres presents the Trust with a major financial responsibility which must continue to be met if future generations are to enjoy its properties. Our forebears have helped give us the Trust as it is today. You can help to protect that inheritance for future generations.

You can help in many different ways:

☐ **LEGACIES**

Legacies of all sizes represent a vital safeguard for the future of The National Trust for Scotland. If you enjoy the Trust please consider leaving a legacy of any amount so that others who follow may have the same pleasure. Legacies are used only on properties and never on administration. You may leave a legacy to support specific properties or areas as you prefer. Alternatively you can leave a legacy to the Trust's discretion. Bequests of property, furniture, etc are equally welcome but it is preferred that you discuss this in confidence with the Trust in the first instance.

☐ **GIFT MEMBERSHIP**

Introduce a member of the family or a friend to the beauty of the Trust. An ideal birthday or Christmas present (see page 86). And don't forget Corporate Membership for businesses.

☐ **DEED OF COVENANT**

Simplicity itself. Please pay your subscription under Deed of Covenant if you are a taxpayer and the Trust will receive an extra 30 per cent in tax relief. Annual donations for more than three years can also be increased in this way.

☐ **GIFT AID**

Any donation of £250 or more by a taxpayer also allows the Trust to recover tax on completion of a simple form by the donor. A gift of £250 becomes worth £324.67!

☐ **SPONSORSHIP**

There are many ways that businesses can sponsor the Trust, from helping with the costs of an education leaflet for children, to contributing towards the improvement of facilities at properties.

For further information please tick the relevant box(es) above, cut out the page and send it to:

The National Trust for Scotland
Development Department
FREEPOST
5 Charlotte Square
Edinburgh
EH2 0DF
or tel (0131) 243 9343; fax (0131) 243 9302;
e-mail funding@nts.org.uk.

Name ....

Address ....

....

.... Postcode ....

Data Protection Act 1998

The personal details you supply here will be held for the purposes specified and for mailing you with information about the NTS. Your details will be used only by the NTS, and will not be made available to any third party. I consent to my details being held for the above purposes.

Signed .... Date ....

Under a 1938 Act of Parliament, The National Trust for Scotland was given the power to make Conservation Agreements with owners of properties the Trust considers worthy of conservation in the national interest. Owners voluntarily agree that no alterations should be made to their properties without the Trust's permission. Ownership remains unaltered, and the agreements continue whoever owns the subjects thereafter. There are now well over 600 such agreements: the main ones are listed here, with the names of those who made them with the Trust (not necessarily the present owners). It excludes all land previously owned by the Trust or where the Trust has feued land or buildings, for example under the Little Houses Improvement Scheme or the Crofting Acts, as all these are secured in this way.

1939 **Nether Pollok,** Glasgow. 1,118 acres. Sir John Stirling Maxwell of Pollok, Bart, KT. (This was the first conservation agreement entered into by the Trust and one of the most important in its history. The generosity of Sir John secured the amenity of open space and woodland for ever 'for the benefit of the citizens of Glasgow' and a more recent Trust initiative led to a site being found for the building to house the Burrell Collection.)

1943 to 1991 **Cally Estate,** Gatehouse-of-Fleet, Galloway. 11,314 acres of low ground, hill and woodland in 17 agreements by Mrs Murray Usher, OBE, of Cally and the Cally Discretionary Trust. ½m coastline.

1944 **West Links,** North Berwick. 122 acres. 1½m coast. The late Col Grant of Biel.

1958 **Cardoness,** Gatehouse-of-Fleet. 370 acres. 1m coast. Mr R W Rainsford-Hannay.

1959 **Glenfinnan,** Highland. 28 acres. Mr A MacKellaig.

1960 **Kinross House,** Kinross. 165 acres. Sir David Montgomery, Bart.

1960 and 1965 **Denburn Park,** Crail. 3 acres. Prof D Rutherford Dow.

1961 **Pentlands** - Allermuir and Caerketton. 270 acres. Major Henry R Trotter.

1962 **Leith Hall** (Lodge Farm). 47 acres. Mr W Massie.

1963 **Craigievar.** 449 acres. Trustees of the late Lord Sempill.

1967 and 1991 **Dunollie,** Oban. 206 acres. 1¼m coast. Madam MacDougall of MacDougall and Miss H MacDougall of MacDougall.

1967 **Grennan,** Rockcliffe. 7 acres. The late Mr and Mrs A D Hopkinson.

1968 **The Whangie.** 492 acres. Mr E S M Collingwood-Cameron.

1970 **Loch Shieldaig,** Highland. 270 acres. 2m coast. Madam Mackenzie of Gairloch.

1970 **Charlotte Square,** Edinburgh. Garden/car park behind the north side. ½ acre. Various owners.

1970 **Durness,** Highland. 580 acres.

5m coast (two agreements). Mr and Mrs T I Robinson.

1971 **Kyle House,** Skye. 24 acres. ½m coast. Mr and Mrs C H Mackenzie.

1971 **Mains of Glinn,** Stirling. 3 acres. Mr J M Colville.

1971 **Dunure,** near Ayr. 5m coastline. (i) Dunure: 18 acres. ½m coast. Lt-Col J K MacFarlan. (ii) Drumshang: 758 acres. 2½m coast. Mr Gavin Morton. (iii) Genoch: 169 acres. 1m coast. Mr Gavin Morton's Children's Trustees. (iv) Drumbain: 96 acres. 1m coast. Mr Alan Carson.

1972 **Beanston Mill,** East Lothian. 1 acre. Mr and Mrs R Cowe.

1972 **West House,** Culross. Miss K Adam.

1972 **Grey Mare's Tail.** 490 acres. Mr J Graham and Forestry Commission.

1972 **Pitmedden** (South Mains). Mr G Barron.

1973 **Skelpick,** Bettyhill. 1,530 acres. 8m coast. Lord Roborough.

1973 **North Berwick.** The Law, East Links, Glen, Lodge Gardens and Harbour. 307 acres. 2m coast. Royal Burgh of North Berwick.

1973 **Tongue, Highland.** 2,600 acres. 10m coast. The Countess of Sutherland.

1973 **Dundonnell,** Highland. 32,500 acres. 34m coast. The late Mr Alan S Roger, Mr Neil M Roger and the late Mr Alastair F R Roger.

1974 **Silverburn,** Leven. 33 acres. Dr David Russell. The Burgh of Leven.

1974 **Cloch Lighthouse** and Houses. ½ acre. Clyde Port Authority. Messrs J Alcorn, John Keogh and Colin S R Crawford.

1974 **Erraid,** Pentlands, Edinburgh. 12 acres. Mrs Ruth Hyde.

1974 **Elie Ness** and Chapelgreen, Fife. 31 acres. 1m coast. The Royal Burgh of Elie and Earlsferry.

1974 **The Merse,** Rockcliffe. (i) Misses D and K Pettigrew; (ii) Mr Abraham; (iii) Trustees of the late Mr J W Munro, Miss C Voge, Mrs V Govan, Mrs V Paterson, Mr T Skinner. Total area 2 acres. ¼m coast.

1975 **Crail,** Fife, The Den. 1 acre. Crail Preservation Society.

1975 **Elie,** Fife. (i) Harbour and granary. 6 acres. ½m coast. The Royal Burgh of Elie and Earlsferry. (ii) Mid-dome. 2 acres. Lady Harvie Watt.

1976 **Castle Fraser,** Grampian. Over 203 acres of the estate around Castle Fraser. Major and Mrs Michael Smiley.

1976 **Inverlael,** Wester Ross. 680 acres. 2m coastline at the head of Loch Broom. Mr S M Whitteridge.

1976 **Wester Kaimes Castle,** Isle of Bute. 3 acres including the castle. The Marquess of Bute.

1976 **Gosford,** East Lothian. 3m of coastline including interesting wind-shaped woodland behind. 196 acres. Trustees of the 12th Earl of Wemyss and March.

1976 **Neidpath Castle,** Peebles. 349 acres of the estate surrounding the

castle. W of Peebles. Trustees of the 12th Earl of Wemyss and March.

1977 **Bluestone House,** Crail. Mr John Young.

1977 **The Old House,** New Abbey. 1 acre. Mr Charles Stewart.

1979 **Wallneuk Cottage,** Cathedral Street, Dunkeld. Mearns Sawmills Ltd.

1979 **Thatched Cottage,** Glamis. Mr C J Sellers.

1980 **Friends Meeting House,** Kinmuck, Grampian. The Rev Dr and Mrs Armstrong.

1980 **Keir Hill,** Gargunnock. 1 acre. The Gargunnock Charitable Trust.

1981 **Greenbank,** Glasgow. 20 acres of fields surrounding the Trust's property. Mr J C K Young.

1981 **Ravenshall,** near Gatehouse-of-Fleet. 24 acres of field and cliff - approximately ½m of coast. The Trustees of Mr R W Rainsford-Hannay. (See also Cardoness.)

1981 **North Lodge,** Dunkeld. 0.4 acres. Lady Smith.

1981 **Green Craig,** Longniddry, East Lothian. 2 acres. Clenex Ltd (by arrangement with the 12th Earl of Wemyss and March).

1983 **Lawers Burn,** Loch Tay. 8 acres. Miss J Meikle.

1984 **Fyvie.** 95 acres of land adjoining the castle. The Trustees of Fyvie Estate and Sir Andrew Forbes-Leith (two agreements).

1984 **Mill Farm,** Gargunnock. 23 acres adjacent to Keir Hill (see above). Trustees of the Gargunnock Estate.

1985 **Dhivach Lodge,** Drumnadrochit. 9 acres. Mrs W C Bowman.

1987 **Luss Village** (part). 4 acres. WHPT Scottish Housing Association Limited.

1988 **Island of Inchmarnock.** 660 acres. 6m coast. Mary-Rose Hamilton Bremner.

1989 **Castle Menzies** and walled garden. 3½ acres. The Menzies Clan Society.

1990 **Coille Mhor Cottage,** Rowardennan. Mrs K E H Smith.

1990 **12 Abercromby Place,** Edinburgh. Mr J F Robertson.

1991 **Land at Rhubodach,** Isle of Bute. 121 acres. 1.8m coast. Sir Richard Attenborough CBE and Lady Sheila Attenborough.

1992 **Castle of Eilean Mhic Chrion,** Ardfern, Argyll. 132 acres. Hazel Mary Hodgkin, Paul Keith Hodgkin and Juliet Kathleen Steer.

1992 **Dunsinane,** Collace. Hill fort and adjoining land. 37.6 acres. James Matheson Sinclair.

1993 **Castle Fraser & Braeneil Farm.** 163.76 acres. M J & A Boughey Ltd.

1994 **Dunollie,** Oban. 3 areas of ground. 0.03 acres. Mrs Morag MacDougall Morley.

1994 **St Abb's Head.** 1.43 acres. Mrs Ruth Roderick Clark.

1994 **St Abb's Head.** 1.08 acres. Mrs Vera Waters.